Are You Ready?

Are You Ready?
T.D. Jakes

DESTINY IMAGE® PUBLISHERS, INC.
P.O. Box 310, Shippensburg, PA 17257-0310
"Promoting Inspired Lives."

This book and all other Destiny Image, Revival Press, Mercy-Place, Fresh Bread, Destiny Image Fiction, and Treasure House books are available at Christian bookstores and distributors worldwide.

For a U.S. bookstore nearest you, call:
1-800-722-6774.
For more information on foreign distributors, call:
717-532-3040.
Or reach us on the Internet: www.destinyimage.com.

ISBN 10: 0-7684-1008-8
ISBN 13: 978-0-7684-1008-2

Previously Published Pneuma Life Publishing
ISBN 1-56229-433-4; Copyright © 1996 by T.D. Jakes.
Previously published as *The Harvest* by Destiny Image Publishers under ISBN 10: 0-7684-2642-1
ISBN 13: 978-0-7684-2642-7

For Worldwide Distribution, Printed in the U.S.A.

1 2 3 4 5 6 7 8 9 10 11 / 16 15 14 13 12

Table of Contents

Foreword

I cannot think of a greater living example of the consistent ability to draw on the anointing of the Lord. T.D. Jakes is man without equal. There is much we can all learn from his words, his spirit and his passion in delivering the Word of the Lord. Just watching him is a wonder in itself. The presence of the Lord flows so freely from him as he teaches. He is simple, clear, and honest in his delivery. Sometimes urgent, sometimes gentle, but always accurate and penetrating. He is a man whose inner focus is on the Lord Himself. Even in his most emotional presentation, you can also see the rest and peace in his eyes. The Holy Spirit will always move freely through those who have no other desire than to give the Word of the Lord to hungry people. And make no mistake about it, God has much to say to His people. He has much He wants to communicate to the world around us. There is much to learn from the Bishop's words, but also his method, his passion, and his love of the Lord Jesus Himself.

I first met the Bishop at a small conference in the Pocono Mountains where he was ministering. That was just before he wrote *Woman, Thou Art Loosed!* We literally walked into each other that fateful afternoon in the basement area of the conference center where vendors were displaying their products. The moment I touched him I prophesied about a book churning in his heart. A few weeks later he called me and the rest, as they say, is history.

There are three criteria we use when determining the possibility of publishing a new author. We look at the person, his message, and his ministry. In the Bishop's case, all three were intricately wrapped with integrity, gentleness, and truth. We are proud to offer this work to the world. He is a man who has allowed the Lord to mold him into a vessel He can use to change the lives of millions around the world. We are grateful to be a part of God's plan for the life of Bishop T.D. Jakes.

Don Nori, Founder
Destiny Image Publishers

Introduction
Where Harvest Begins

*Another parable put He forth unto them,
saying, The kingdom of heaven is likened
unto a man which sowed good seed in
his field: but while men slept, his enemy
came and sowed tares among the wheat,
and went his way. But when the blade
was sprung up, and brought forth fruit,
then appeared the tares also. So the servants of the householder came and said
unto him, Sir, didst not thou sow good
seed in thy field? from whence then hath
it tares? He said unto them, an enemy*

hath done this. The servants said unto him, wilt thou then that we go and gather them up? But he said, Nay; lest while ye gather up the tares, ye root up also the wheat with them. Let both grow together until the harvest: and in the time of harvest I will say to the reapers, Gather ye together first the tares, and bind them in bundles to burn them: but gather the wheat into my barn (Matthew 13:24-30).

Throughout the history of Israel, harvest represented a time of great jubilation. The Hebrews recognized the reaping of the harvest as God's provision for the months to come. It was also the time to pay off old debts. For those who loaned other people money, harvest time meant pay day. The harvest also provided many of the essential herbs that were used for natural healing. In light of this, we can understand Jeremiah's disappointment and discouragement that harvest time for Israel had come and gone:

The harvest is past, the summer is ended, and we are not saved. Is there no balm in Gilead; is there no physician there? Why then is not the health of the daughter of my people recovered? (Jeremiah 8:20,22).

The people of Israel were in the same condition, if not worse than before the harvest.

Is that where we are in America today?

We had the Azusa Street revival, early in this century, and the healing evangelist movement that began in the late 1940s. During the 1960s, the social revival with Martin Luther King swept the nation. The 1970s brought the charismatic renewal and the Word of Faith movement that continued into the early and mid-80s. Lastly, we have experienced the resurgence of the prophetic voice in the early 1990s and more recently the Toronto Blessing.

Much like the predicament faced by the prophet Jeremiah, however, Christians, particularly in America, find themselves wondering, Why is our nation still sick with sin and violence?

Many harvests have passed, and our nation as a whole is still spiritually destitute. We have more death and destruction than ever before. Crime is rampant in our streets, and the divorce rate is at an all-time high with one out of every two marriages breaking up.

To many, homosexuality has become an acceptable alternative lifestyle. Racism, though more sophisticated and attitudinal, is as prevalent

13

as it was more than 40 years ago, before the signing of the Civil Rights Bill.

The most troubling reality about America's social and moral condition, however, is that there is just as much sin and hopelessness inside the Church as outside.

The Starting Place

Why is our nation so lacking in moral character and stability? People blame everything and everybody from politics to parents, from ungodly music to the media but no one is willing to take responsibility for the moral decay in our society. No one is willing to take the blame for the problems we now face. To make matters worse, no one is offering any viable, long-lasting solutions.

God, however, knows exactly who is responsible for the breakdown and corrosion of the moral fiber and godly ethic of our nation. The responsible party is none other than the Church. And that is where God plans to start.

> *For the time is come that judgment must begin at the house of God: and if it first begin at us, what shall the end be of them that obey not the gospel of God?* (1 Peter 4:17).

God has placed the Church in the earth to be a representative and an advocate of His will. Without a righteous standard, there is no parameter for God to use in judging the unrighteous works of wicked men and women. Judgment must always first begin with the house of God because God's people are supposed to be a vivid and conspicuous example of the will of God on earth.

We should thank God that judgment begins in the house of the Lord. Why? Because politicians can't turn our nation around; law enforcement agencies can't prevent violence and hatred; and schools can't change children's hearts. All man's efforts are futile when it comes to getting right with God.

When the Church holds up the righteous standard, we can then work with God to help our families, friends, communities, schools, and cities. Eventually the nation will get right with God, and justice, morality, and righteousness will return. God has even provided the formula for getting right with Him:

If My people, which are called by My name, shall humble themselves, and pray, and seek my face, and turn from their wicked ways; then will I hear from heaven, and will forgive their sin, and will heal their land (2 Chronicles 7:14).

God expects His people, those called by His name, who claim to be a part of the Body of Christ, to humble themselves. That means He wants us to stop being so judgmental, condemning, critical, and at the same time hypocritical. Then, He promises to forgive our sin.

God didn't say He would forgive the sin of the world; He said He would forgive the sin of His people, the chosen, the Church Christians.

After the Church repents for the sins of the nation, then and only then will God hear our cry for revival and reconciliation. First, we, the Church, must repent of our own wickedness and our hardened hearts. We must ask forgiveness for our insensitivity to the pain and heartache of those in the world around—us those lost without hope and without Christ.

When the Church in America repents for the sins of America past and present then will God be gracious to us and forgive our sins and heal our land.

Chapter 1
Your Last Chance?

Your Last Chance?

The coming harvest has two phases. The first harvest involves believers who are being gathered together to inherit eternal life. The second phase includes the wicked who are being bundled together for the purpose of destruction.

Those not living according to the will of God and disobeying His laws are going to hell. No doubt about it!

"That sounds like hellfire and brimstone preaching," you say, "and I really don't care to hear it!"

As a minister of the gospel of Jesus Christ, I am required to preach the truth. Whether sinners accept it or not, is not my concern. The preacher's responsibility to God and man is to live and preach the revealed Word of God.

When I say unto the wicked, O wicked man, thou shalt surely die; if thou dost not speak to warn the wicked from his way, that wicked man shall die in his iniquity; but his blood will I require at thine hand. Nevertheless, if thou warn the wicked of his way to turn from it; if he do not turn from his way, he shall die in his iniquity; but thou hast delivered thy soul (Ezekiel 33:8-9).

As a preacher of the good news of the saving grace of God, I am called to preach the message of the cross (see 1 Cor. 2:1-2) and the power of the resurrected life (see Phil. 3:10) that has been made available through the life, death, burial, and resurrection of the only begotten Son of God, the Lord Jesus Christ. If a sinner hears this message and refuses to repent, the consequence becomes his loss and not my responsibility.

As ministers of reconciliation (see 2 Cor. 5:18), we must speak the truth, and do so in love (see Eph. 4:15). It is the goodness of God that leads people to repentance (see Rom. 2:4) not the wrath of God, and assuredly not the wrath of humankind (see James 1:20).

Under the leading and inspiration of the Holy Spirit, when we, as ministers of the gospel, have preached as sincerely and effectively as possible, all who hear are then accountable to God for what they have heard. It becomes their responsibility not to simply be hearers of the Word of God, but doers also (see James 1:22).

The Choice Is Yours

Once people have heard the truth and still fail to submit and comply with God's Word, they are, in the eyes of Almighty God, without excuse.

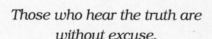

Those who hear the truth are without excuse.

As a born-again Christian, you also must submit and obey the truth or suffer the consequences. Like the unregenerate sinner, you are absolutely without excuse in the face of the truth of the Word of God. You are required to act on what you know, because to whom much is given much is required. (See Luke 12:48.)

You won't be able to say, "Lord, I didn't know lying (or adultery or greed or whatever) was wrong."

The Lord will reply, "Remember that old country preacher who preached to you that day with sweat rolling down his face? He told you I was getting ready to do what I had promised through the prophets of old. But you ignored My Word and did not heed My warnings. You had a chance to repent and turn from your wicked ways."

God is not a man, that He should lie; neither the son of man, that He should repent: hath He said, and shall He not do it? or hath He spoken, and shall He not make it good? (Numbers 23:19).

In other words, God is not wishy-washy. He is not moved by your whining and complaining. His ways are clearly spelled out in His Word. You can choose either to obey or disobey.

The God of the Second Chance

The heavenly Father is always willing to give His unrepentant children the opportunity to turn to Him completely, without reservation or restriction. All we have to do is confess our sins before Him, assured that He is "faithful and just to forgive us our sins, and to cleanse us from all unrighteousness" (1 John 1:9).

God's desire is not to condemn, but to redeem.

There is therefore now no condemnation to them which are in Christ Jesus, who walk not after the flesh, but after the Spirit. For the law of the Spirit of life in Christ Jesus hath made me free from the law of sin and death (Romans 8:1-2).

God is always willing to forgive and restore, as long as He knows that we are sincere and that our hearts are open toward Him.

King David, an adulterer and a murderer, repented of his sin and found God's loving kindness and His mercies new every morning.

Be merciful unto me, O Lord: for I cry unto Thee daily. For Thou, Lord, art good, and ready to forgive; and plenteous in mercy unto all them that call upon Thee. For great is Thy mercy toward me: and Thou hast delivered my soul from the lowest hell. But Thou, O Lord, art a God full of compassion, and gracious, long-suffering, and plenteous in mercy and truth (Psalm 86:3,5,13,15).

God's love toward His children is so great that He continues to stretch forth His hand, extending it the second, third, and fourth time, until we get our hearts right with Him.

> *God is truly a God of second chances.*

All I needed was a chance. When I heard the Word of God speaking to my heart to come out of the world, I climbed out of sin in a hurry. When I told my friends good-bye, they laughed at me. In fact, they continue to mock my ministry, imitating the way I praise and worship God.

That doesn't bother me, because the same Holy Spirit I received years ago, is still real and present in my life today. He keeps me alive, holy, and righteous before God without blame!

While my friends are shooting up, snorting drugs, getting arrested, going to jail, and living in sin, I'm free, shouting and praising God. I'm enjoying the liberty, joy, and peace of abundant life in the Lord Jesus Christ. I'm happily married, raising godly children, prospering, and going forth proclaiming the gospel.

When God blesses you, not only will He bless you personally, but He will bless your family, your field, your crops, and your land. According to Deuteronomy 28, God will take you who used to be the tail and make you the head.

When all of your former friends are miserable and dying with needles in their arms, you can have joy in your heart, peace in your mind, and victory over the lust of the flesh. God, and God alone, can and will do that for you. He is the God of the second chance.

With or Without Christ?

Many people, because of certain accomplishments and worldly success, have become self-deceived into believing that their success is exclusively the result of their own skill and hard work. I hate to be the one to burst their bubbles, but it is not so.

If you want to experience the best that life has to offer, you must, sooner or later, realize that without God's leading, guiding, counseling, and empowering, you can do nothing.

---

*To experience life's best,
you need God.*

You may say, "I know people who are not saved and not serving God, yet they're doing this and they've done that."

By the world's standards, their accomplishments may appear impressive, but in the eyes of God they mean nothing. It is all in vain.

Remember, it is only what you do for Christ that will last. Regardless of what you achieve or acquire here on earth, if it's not according to God's will and purpose for your life, it means absolutely nothing.

The apostle Paul said that all he had gained or accomplished before submitting his life to Christ, he now considered to be "dung" (Phil. 3:8). In other words, he said, "What a waste!"

What good is it to gain the whole world and lose your own soul?

Jesus said:

Abide in Me, and I in you. As the branch cannot bear fruit of itself, except it abide in the vine; no more can ye, except ye abide in Me. I am the vine, ye are the branches: He that abideth in Me, and I in him, the same bringeth forth much fruit: for without Me ye can do nothing (John 15:4-5).

You need the Lord. Whether you want Him or not, you need God. More than you need your credit card, your car keys, or your paycheck, you need to be one with Christ Jesus!

I'm not talking about religion, or going to church and putting your name on an aristo-cratic roll. I'm talking about having your soul washed in the crucified blood of Jesus Christ, the only begotten Son of the only true and liv-ing God.

A Weak Argument

Sinners and backslidden Christians often blame their failure to submit and yield their lives totally to God on the hypocritical, con-demning, and un-Christlike behavior of the Christians they have met. In spite of their dis-illusionment and the fact that some so-called Christians may act in ways that do not glorify God, no one is absolved from their own per-sonal responsibility to act on the revealed Word of God.

The apostle Paul made this clear in his let-ter to the Roman Christians:

For the wrath of God is revealed from heaven against all ungodliness and unrighteousness of men, who hold the truth in unrighteousness; because that which may be known of God is manifest in them; for God hath shewed it unto them. For the invisible things of Him from the creation of the world are clearly seen, being understood by the things that are made, even His eternal power and God-head; so that they are without excuse... (Romans 1:18-20).

Sinners must understand that regardless of the behavior of some Christians, they are still without excuse. They will still be judged for their refusal to accept Christ as their Lord and Savior and their failure to believe on the name of the only begotten Son of God.

For God sent not His Son into the world to condemn the world; but that the world through Him might be saved. He that believeth on him is not condemned: but he that believeth not is condemned already, because he hath not believed in the name of the only begotten Son of God (John 3:17-18).

No one can say they did not have adequate knowledge of God and what He requires, as the Amplified version of the Bible makes plain:

For ever since the creation of the world His invisible nature and attributes, that is, His eternal power and divinity, have been made intelligible and clearly discernible in and through the things that have been made (His handiworks). So [men] are without excuse [altogether without any defense or justification] (Romans 1:20 AMP).

The glory and majesty of God is manifest by the natural elements, as the psalmist reveals:

The heavens declare the glory of God; and the firmament sheweth His handywork. Day unto day uttereth speech, and night unto night sheweth knowledge. There is no speech nor language, where their voice is not heard (Psalm 19:1-3).

Seeing the wonders of God should cause us to consider the awesomeness of God and how we, as humans, fit into His divine scheme of things. Observing the balance of the universe should lead us to conclude there is no one like

There is no one like God; His existence demands worship.

God, and His very existence demands that we worship Him while we live on His earth.

Humanism is no more than man's feeble attempt to put himself on God's level. Only a sinful man, however, would be foolish enough to do so.

The apostle Paul describes people who claim to be religious but refuse to worship God:

> ...*When they knew God, they glorified Him not as God, neither were thankful; but became vain in their imaginations, and their foolish heart was darkened. Professing themselves to be wise, they became fools* (Romans 1:21-22).

If Not Now, When?

Wouldn't it be terrible to discover there had been a time of great and wonderful harvest, and you, through ignorance and disobedience, were not part of it?

Nothing creates more regret than knowing something wonderful happened and realizing that you missed it. "I was about to turn my life around; I was thinking about giving my life to God, but I just acted too late."

Maybe you even expressed to friends and relatives, "You know, I have been thinking about getting saved!"

But when they laughed and said, "You're just playing the religious game," you decided at the last minute not to commit your life to Jesus.

Now you find yourself lost and without God.

"I was thinking about it," you say, "but there are some things I want to do first, some pleasures I haven't yet experienced."

With deep regret, you wonder, "I don't know why I didn't come to the Lord. I had an opportunity to give my heart to Jesus, and I just sat there on the verge of yielding. I felt like it. I even grabbed the front of the pew; I started to stand up. I don't know why I didn't. I don't know what kept me in my seat, but I thought it was too soon. Maybe next week."

You waited, and now the harvest has passed.

Jeremiah, declared, "The harvest is passed, the summer is ended, and [still] we are not saved" (Jer. 8:20).

31

Sinner-man or woman, boy or girl, don't miss this harvest. Don't let it pass you by! You may never get another chance. Another harvest may not knock at your door again. Arise *now* and give your life to Jesus Christ.

Don't miss this harvest!

Thoughts and Reflections

Chapter 2
A Question of Life or Death

A Question of Life or Death

In Matthew chapter 13, Jesus told the parable of a good man who sowed good seed in his field, but during the night his enemy came and sowed tares among the wheat. As the plants grew, it became obvious that wheat-like imitations were cropping up along with the wheat.

The sower's servants asked the householder, "Didn't you sow good seed in the field? But now we see all of this corruption. Where did these weeds come from?"

The kingdom of heaven is likened unto a man which sowed good seed in his field:

But while men slept, his enemy came and sowed tares among the wheat, and went his way. But when the blade was sprung up, and brought forth fruit, then appeared the tares also. So the servants of the householder came and said unto him, Sir, didst not thou sow good seed in thy field? from whence then hath it tares? (Matthew 13:24-27)

In interpreting this parable, Jesus told His disciples, "He that soweth the good seed is the Son of man..." (Matt. 13:37). When Jesus, by His Holy Spirit, sows a seed, it's a good seed.

What is "the seed"? The Word of God is the seed that when planted in the fertile ground of a person's heart brings forth spiritual life. When the spiritual seed of God's Word germinates, it results in conception, and conception carried to full term results in the birth of a child of God.

The apostle James says that God, of His own will, gave spiritual birth to us who are the sons of God by "the word of truth, that we should be a kind of firstfruits of His creatures" (James 1:18).

When we become born again by the Spirit of God, we become new creatures, or new creations:

"old things are passed away" and "all things are become new" (2 Cor. 5:17). We are new creations in Christ Jesus.

Once the seed of God has been planted in your heart, you can be assured that no matter what the enemy attempts to plant in your life thereafter, it will (as long as you are faithful to God) never entirely alter the fruit that springs forth from God's pure seed.

> *Once the seed of God is planted, nothing can alter it.*

Being born again, not of corruptible seed, but of incorruptible, by the word of God, which liveth and abideth forever (1 Peter 1:23).

God's Word is pure, and once you are born again God will guard and protect the pure seed He has planted in your heart. He will watch over His Word "to perform it" (Jer. 1:12).

Being a born-again believer in the Lord Jesus is not the same as being a member of any particular religion. Being a son of God and member of the Body of Christ is not dependent upon joining or being accepted by the denomination of choice.

Jesus put it this way: In order to become a citizen of the kingdom of God, "You must be born again!" (See John 3:5.)

Getting to the Heart of the Problem

When people join a particular religion, they are often seeking to fill a void, or to change their behavior and general outlook on life. This is usually accomplished by some form of behavior modification, such as abstaining from certain meats, wearing certain clothes, and the exercising and keeping of certain rituals and rules. This like the keeping of the Law of Moses is referred to as "legal-ism."

As Christians, however, we should not be bound by rules and regulations, as the apostle Paul explained to the believers at Colosse:

Wherefore if ye be dead with Christ from the rudiments of the world, why, as though living in the world, are ye subject to ordinances, (touch not; taste not; handle not; which all are to perish with the using;) after the commandments and doctrines of men? (Colossians 2:20-22).

Without the Spirit of God abiding in one's heart, keeping such laws and rituals is actually impossible. God's Word says in James 2:10 that "whosoever shall keep the whole law, and yet offend in one point, he is guilty of all." If you break one law, you are guilty of breaking all the laws.

Attempting to keep laws and rituals only changes the outward man, not the eternal, hidden man of the heart. And our heart is where the problem begins.

"The heart is deceitful above all things, and desperately wicked" (Jer. 17:9). Wickedness is bred into the very fiber of man's soul, as Psalm 51:5 makes clear: "Behold, I was shapen in iniquity; and in sin did my mother conceive me."

The apostle Paul explained to the Roman believers that by the sin of the first man, Adam, all have sinned and entered into death: "Wherefore, as by one man sin entered into the world, and death by sin; and so death passed upon all men, for that all have sinned" (Rom. 5:12). As a result, "There is none righteous, no, not one.... For all have sinned, and come short of the glory of God" (Rom. 3:10, 23).

In order to be righteous, man needs more than a temporary change in his external behavior. Man needs a change of heart—a new heart:

And I will give them one heart, and I will put a new spirit within you; and I will take the stony heart out of their flesh, and will give them an heart of flesh: That they may walk in My statutes, and keep Mine ordinances, and do them: and they shall be My people and I will be their God (Ezekiel 11:19-20).

Such transformation can only take place supernaturally by the impartation of the Word of God. That is why King David declared, "Thy word have I hid in mine heart, that I might not sin against thee" (Ps. 119:11). When the seed of the Word, the life of God, abides in the believer:

Whosoever is born of God doth not commit sin; for His seed remaineth in him: and he cannot commit sin, because he is born of God (1 John 3:9).

---

*Where the life of God abides,
sin loses its power.*

This doesn't mean if you are born again, you will never sin in the flesh. It does mean if you are truly born of the incorruptible seed of the Word of God, you no longer remain a slave to sin. In the life of the born-again, Spirit-filled believer, sin no longer has dominion not even over the mortal body. Sin doesn't control you; instead, you, by the power of God's Spirit, control sin.

Death Before Life

Today, we seldom hear biblical teaching that emphasizes the death of the flesh by way of the cross. As a result, the Church is in danger of becoming like those whom the apostle Paul called enemies of the cross of Christ (see Phil. 3:18).

Jesus, however, repeatedly stressed the importance of dying to self. He said:

> *Verily, verily, I say unto you, Except a corn of wheat fall into the ground and die, it abideth alone: but if it die, it bringeth forth much fruit* (John 12:24).

When a seed is planted in the soil, the life germinating within it cannot spring forth until the outer shell of the seed dies off. There, within the dark, damp earth, new life pushes out of its shell, up through the soil, and into the sunlight, where it grows into a plant and begins to produce fruit.

The Word of God declares that seeds produce after their own kind. Whatever is sown in the ground is what comes up. If a corn seed is planted, it will come up as corn on the cob. Likewise, if an apple seed is sown, it will grow into an apple tree.

Accordingly, Jesus Christ, our seed of righteousness, was buried in the ground three days for the salvation of our souls.

> *Know ye not, that so many of us as were baptized into Jesus Christ were baptized into His death? Therefore we are buried with Him by baptism into death: that like as Christ was raised from the dead by the glory of the Father, even so we also should walk in newness of life. For if we have been planted together in the likeness of His death, we shall be also in the likeness of His resurrection* (Romans 6:3-5).

Christ arose on the third day with all power over sin and death, becoming the Seed of eternal life for all who are willing to believe and call on His name. Everyone who believes, rises up with Him to live in newness of life, now and forever.

I am a product of God. Jesus Christ died that I might have life. By the impartation of the Word of God, the Spirit of Christ was made manifest in my spirit. Through the Holy Spirit my soul is sanctified, thereby making me not just a servant, but a legitimate son of God and an heir of salvation.

The Key to Victorious Living

Scripture is very clear on this issue of "flesh death" and "spirit resurrection." There can be no life without death.

The apostle Paul knew this death to the flesh was so crucial to a victorious Christian life that it became the cry of his heart:

That I may know Him, and the power of His resurrection, and the fellowship of His sufferings, being made conformable unto His death (Philippians. 3:10).

Some Christians like to quote only the first part of this verse, "That I may know Him, and the power of His resurrection," conveniently omitting the remaining portion. They recoil at the thought of knowing Christ in "the fellowship of His sufferings, being made conformable unto His death." (Phil. 3:10b)

You cannot partake of the power of Christ's resurrection unless you are first willing to lay down your own will and desires, and die to all your pride and independence.

Jesus clearly stated:

He that loveth his life shall lose it; and he that hateth his life in this world shall keep it unto life eternal. If any man serve Me, let him follow Me; and where I am, there shall also My servant be: if any man serve Me, him will My Father honour (John 12:25-26).

Unless the believer is willing to lose his life for Christ's sake, he can never attain everlasting life. If the Master must suffer to the point of death, so likewise must the servant.

If the Master must suffer, so likewise must the servant.

If you're going to live a victorious life, as well as experience and enjoy the power of God in your life, you must do as Jesus commanded and deny yourself, take up your cross daily and follow Him.

And He said to them all, If any man will

*come after Me, let him deny himself, and
take up his cross daily, and follow Me.
For whosoever will save his life shall lose
it: but whosoever will lose his life for My
sake, the same shall save it. For what is
a man advantaged, if he gain the whole
world, and lose himself, or be cast away?*
(Luke 9:23-25)

When people read Christian books and listen to sermons and teachings, they are usually
seeking some type of remedy or solution to a
particular pressing issue in life.

If you are searching for the secret of true joy,
and victorious Holy Spirit-filled Christ living, the
answer is simply this: Die! Die and keep on
dying daily until all of you is dead and only
Christ lives. Death is the key to life and life more
abundantly.

Leave It Alone!

When the servants asked the householder
what to do about the strange tares coming up
in the field, he said, "Leave them alone until the
time of harvest."

*So the servants of the householder came
and said unto him, Sir, didst not thou sow
good seed in thy field? From whence then*

hath it tares? He said unto them, An enemy hath done this. The servants saith unto him, Wilt thou then that we go and gather them up? But he said, Nay; lest while ye gather up the tares, ye root up also the wheat with them. Let both grow together until the harvest... (Matthew 13:27-30).

Has something unusual and unpleasant sprung up in your life like an unwanted weed? Has it captured and diverted your attention from God's agenda?

God says, "Leave it alone!" He does not want you to be preoccupied or consumed with this distraction at the present time. "Wait until the time of harvest," He says.

God realizes that satanism is having a revival. He knows that the dispersion of illegal drugs and the violence in America's streets is at an all-time high.

The worldwide spread of new incurable diseases like AIDS has not caught Him off-guard.

Unpleasant situations or undesirable personal issues that you did not expect and did not have any hand in causing what may have developed in your life. Such puzzling and unpredictable problems have the potential to distract and move you away from what God is demanding of you right now.

When faced with such situations, we must "cast our cares upon the Lord" (see 1 Peter 5:7). This doesn't mean we should be lazy and irresponsible concerning the affairs of this world. No. We must truly make Jesus Lord of our lives and believe that God is ultimately in control.

Certain challenges and issues will not be fully resolved or overcome until the fulfillment of their purpose has occurred in our lives. We are admonished in Scripture "to let patience have her perfect work, that ye may be perfect and entire, wanting nothing" (James 1:4).

Simply put, there are things in our lives that are not going to be changed until the time of our personal harvest.

The wise preacher, Solomon, said in the writings of Ecclesiastes:

> *To every thing there is a season, and a time to every purpose under the heaven: A time to be born, and a time to die; a time to plant, and a time to pluck up that which is planted* (Ecclesiastes 3:1-2).

Job said, "All the days of my appointed time will I wait, till my change come" (Job 14:14).

There are certain permanent changes that will not be fully executed in our lives until the time of harvest. When that time comes, God will conclude and fulfill every void and set right the wrongs we had to endure during our spiritual winter season. You may have wondered: Why doesn't God set things right sooner?

First of all, God has a divinely ordained purpose for the problems that evolve in our lives. For every affliction and persecution in the life of the Christian believer, there is a God-prescribed purpose. The hand that molds us to become a person who will manifest the character and fruit of the Spirit is the hand of affliction—the right hand of trial and the left hand of tribulation.

> *The hand of affliction*
> *molds character.*

The Canvas of Confusion

God shows the excellency of His power against the canvas of confusion. In other words, if all of the conditions necessary for being blessed were comfortable and pleasurable, we would praise the conditions and not praise God, the source of the blessing.

When all of the conditions are adverse and it seems there is no way for us to be blessed, and yet we are blessed anyway, what do we do? We praise God who goes beyond conditions and blesses us in spite of circumstances and in spite of our unworthiness to deserve being blessed.

Until the time of harvest, we must endure certain situations and bondages in our lives that have to be continually overcome. If we encounter situations that seem to get the best of us, we must not become despondent. Even in the midst of trials and tribulations, we can still overcome by the blood of the Lamb and the word of our testimony (see Rev. 12:11).

The Bible says when we have "done all, to stand" (Eph. 6:13). David prayed, "Thy word have I hid in mine heart, that I might not sin against Thee" (Ps. 119:11).

If we have been diligent to hide the Word of God in our hearts, and if we continue to labor over that Word, we can be assured that in the time of harvest we will reap a bountiful reward if we faint not. (See Galatians 6:9.)

God has predestined a particular and pre-determined time that He is going to fulfill all the unfulfilled prophecies, tighten up all the loose ends of life, and make the valleys flat and the crooked places straight.

Eventually, all the seemingly terrible events of your life will fit into the scheme of God's divine omniscient plan. When He unveils the completed picture, it will appear, not as a canvas of confusion, but as a perfect portrait of His love for you.

Thoughts and Reflections

_____

_____

_____

_____

_____

_____

_____

_____

_____

_____

_____

_____

_____

_____

_____

_____

_____

_____

_____

Chapter 3
Bundled to Burn

Bundled to Burn

W hy did the householder in Jesus' parable tell the servants to leave the tares intact until the time of harvest? This wise farmer knew that impostor plants were growing among his prized wheat. Still, he told his servants to let them grow together.

But he said, Nay; lest while ye gather up the tares, ye root up also the wheat with them. Let both grow together until the harvest: and in the time of harvest I will say to the reapers, Gather ye together first the tares, and bind them in bundles to burn them: but gather the wheat into my barn (Matthew 13:29-30).

Like the householder, God knows what is going on in the fields He is preparing for harvest. He is aware of the hypocrisy and false heretical tares in the Body of Christ. It comes as no surprise to Him that not every churchgoer is actually a part of the true Body of Christ.

As the Church endeavors to prepare for the time of harvest, we must understand there are two types of harvests taking place. There is a harvest of those souls whose hearts have been made vulnerable for the reception of the gospel. Just prior to this end-time harvest of souls, however, another harvest will occur. It will pluck up the tares that have developed in the Church as a result of false, erroneous, and heretical teaching and doctrine.

Jesus, in explaining the parable of the tares, said:

The Son of man shall send forth His angels, and they shall gather out of His kingdom all things that offend, and them which do iniquity; and shall cast them into a furnace of fire: there shall be wailing and gnashing of teeth (Matthew 13:41-42).

The reaping of this corrupt fruit and dead works will take place *before* the time of wheat harvest, when the true believers are gathered.

Jesus said, "Then shall the righteous shine forth as the sun in the kingdom of their Father. Who hath ears to hear, let him hear" (Matt. 13:43).

Who Are the Tares?

The householder of the field instructed his servants to allow both the wheat and the tares to grow together until the time of harvest. Then he planned to call forth the reapers to gather the tares together in bundles to be burned.

Wheat was reaped either by using a sickle or pulling up the plants by their roots before binding them in sheaths.

In order to comprehend what Jesus is implying by the reaping of tares, we must first understand the nature of tares and their effect upon growing wheat. A tare is a weed referred to as darnel, which, in its early stages, looks very similar, almost identical to wheat.

Darnel only appears distinguishable from wheat when it becomes almost fully grown. At that point, however, the roots of the plant have become so intertwined with the wheat that to pluck them up would be all but impossible to do without destroying the wheat. That's why the householder instructed the servants to let both the wheat and the tares grow until the time of harvest.

When the disciples asked Jesus to explain parable of the tares of the field, He said:

He that soweth the good seed is the Son of man; the field is the world; the good seed are the children of the kingdom; but the tares are the children of the wicked one; The enemy that sowed them is the devil; the harvest is the end of the world; and the reapers are the angels. As therefore the tares are gathered and burned in the fire; so shall it be in the end of this world (Matthew 13:37-40).

The one who sowed the good seed was the Son of man, which is Jesus Christ. The seed represents the Word of God. Those who are the true sons of God are those born by the incorruptible seed of the Word of God. But the children of the wicked one are conceived by the erroneous and false teaching inspired by the devil.

> *True sons of God are born by incorruptible seed.*

The Bible says in the endtimes, or latter days, "some shall depart from the faith, giving heed to seducing spirits, and doctrines of devils; speaking lies in hypocrisy; having their conscience seared with a hot iron" (1 Tim. 4:1-2). These, Jesus said, will be "gathered and burned in the fire" (Matt. 13:40).

In the last days, many who appear to be members of the Body of Christ and sons of God are actually bastards. As children of the devil, these men and women have been seduced by the erroneous doctrines of false teachers and prophets who, according to the apostle Paul, preach "another gospel." (See Second Corinthians 11:4.)

This is true in the Church today. Many contemporary doctrines are absolutely contrary to the words of Christ and the teachings of His apostles. These false doctrines emphasize gratifying the lust of the flesh, in contrast to the death that comes through the cross. Their proponents are more concerned with approval and validation of the world, instead of the approval and accreditation of God the Father.

One such false teaching implies that the more material and monetary things you possess, the more spiritually and morally worthwhile you become. They reach this conclusion by reinterpreting Luke 12:15 to read, "The worth of a man consists in and of the things he possesses," replacing the true, literal meaning that says we are to, "Take heed, and beware of covetousness: for a man's life consisteth *not* in the abundance of the things which he possesseth."

God has given us our measure of faith (see Rom. 12:3) to submit to Him, do His will, and further His kingdom here on earth. We are not to use our faith to pursue our own personal agendas and build our own kingdoms.

Spiritual Poison

Like the tares of the field that resemble the wheat, false teachings are usually similar to the truth. Their deceptions are so subtle that many people cannot discern the difference between their hidden lies and the truth.

> *Like tares that resemble wheat,*
> *false teachings resemble truth.*

These false teachings, in most cases, appear to confess Jesus verbally, but they do not submit to Christ's Lordship. Centered on selfish ambition and personal agendas, they ignore the will and purpose of God for humankind.

Ministers who propagate these erroneous beliefs and philosophies are most commonly greed-oriented, preaching the gospel for monetary and personal gain, rather than for the love of God. Christians who follow such preachers are quick to talk about the power of Christ's resurrection, but avoid at all costs the fellowship of His sufferings.

The apostle Paul called them "enemies of the cross of Christ: whose end is destruction, whose God is their belly, and whose glory is in their shame, who mind earthly things" (Phil. 3:18b-19). "Belly," in this case, symbolizes the dictates of the flesh.

Such fleshly, carnal, worldly Christians use their faith more for acquiring physical and material things rather than believing God for the grace that is necessary to conform them into the image of Christ. Why are they like this? Because they have been beguiled and bewitched by another gospel. They have lost affection for their first love, Christ, and have become subjected to the dictates of the world, instead of yielding to the demands of the Spirit of the Almighty God.

Vine's Expository Dictionary of Biblical Words states that the seed of darnel (tares) are "poisonous to man" and can produce "sleepiness, nausea, convulsions and even death." Such characteristics are true of the effects of false teachings upon the souls of Christians.

Duped into slumber by poisonous doctrines, they are lazy and complacent when it comes to reaching the lost for Christ. Like the effects of darnel, these types of so-called saints have become spiritually nauseated, unable to digest even the sincere milk of the Word of God. For them, attempting to partake of the meat of God's Word is out of the question.

Like the most destructive consequence of consuming the tare darnel, some Christians are walking around spiritually dead and don't even know it. The apostle Paul said some are sick and even asleep (dead) because they have failed to rightly discern the Body of Christ:

> *For he that eateth and drinketh unworthily, eateth and drinketh damnation to himself, not discerning the Lord's body. For this cause many are weak and sickly among you, and many sleep* (1 Corinthians 11:29-30).

This is why some churches, conferences, evangelistic crusades, and even so-called revivals have no life in them. The people have become sick and infected with the spirit of the tares. Because they have not learned how to rightly discern the will of God, these Christians are sometimes sick unto death.

The Bundling Together

As we approach the era of the end-time harvest, the separation of good and evil will become more and more apparent. This will be especially obvious in the Church as people gravitate toward their own kind.

If a group of people gather in a room, all of the liars will eventually find each other. You do not have to put a sign on them to indicate to other potential liars that there are liars present. The liars will gravitate toward one another automatically.

All the gossipers will avoid the praying people; they do not want to be around anyone who is too godly. Gossipers immediately detect who is and who is not a gossiper. Soon they find old slick-tongue Sally and get together in bundles for a lying, gossiping good time while trying to give the impression they are praying, of course.

Eventually, all the phonies and the troublemakers find each other and get on the same auxiliary boards.

All of the homosexual spirits know and recognize one another. When they enter a room, they automatically sense each other without ever being introduced. They can look into an individual's eyes and know if he or she is of the same spirit. Onlookers cannot tell what's going on, but the homosexuals will intuitively know each other. Soon all the lesbians get together and form groups and cliques.

Like kind begets like kind. Evil attracts evil; wickedness attracts wickedness; perversion attracts perversion. In the endtime, however, God will be the One gathering them into bundles to be burned.

Some people, no matter how much you preach and teach them, refuse to change. They will dance all over the church, shout, and holler all day and night long, but when the choir has stopped singing and the preacher has stopped preaching, they will go right back to doing what they were doing before.

Why? Because they are children of the evil one, waiting to be gathered in bundles to be burned.

Like kind begets like kind.

They are more comfortable in their bundles than they are in being part of the end-time harvest. They enjoy their sin and want to be bound.

Keep your eyes and ears open. In these latter days, there is going to be a bundling together of false doctrines, false spirits, and false mentalities that are contrary to the Spirit, will, and Word of God.

Separated to Be Burned

The householder in Jesus' parable did not tell the servants to burn the tares while they were in the field alongside the righteous wheat.

Gather ye together first the tares, and bind them in bundles to burn them: but gather the wheat into my barn (Matthew 13:30).

He said, "First gather them together so they can be burned away from the wheat. Set them apart so the burning will not harm the wheat, which is already white to harvest."

The householder didn't say burn them first and then gather them together to be bundled. No! He said first gather the tares together so they can be bundled individually, separate and distinctive from the wheat.

These tares, children of the evil one, don't even know they are being gathered together to be burned. They don't realize that their fatal attraction is drawing them to each other in preparation for burning. While they mock the true saints of God, these evil ones are unaware that they are being gathered together for destruction.

God is getting ready to wrap up the world as we know it. We're coming to the end of this era of time. Now, as never before, it is time to get right with God. You need to do it now.

I'm not worried about hurting your feelings or offending your carnal flesh. My concern is that you will understand, while you can, the truth and urgency of what the Spirit of God is saying to the Church in these last and pivotal times.

God is quickly fulfilling today all that He has said in the past through His prophets, and is speaking presently through His ministers and servants. We are embarking upon the time of harvest.

Jesus didn't apologize when He said "them which do iniquity will be cast into a furnace of fire: there shall be wailing and gnashing of teeth" (see Matt. 13:41-42).

In this time of harvest, God is saying, "I'm going to gather the wickedness of My Church and the world together into bundles to be burned—to be destroyed by fire hellfire."

No Compromise

For those who want to be delivered from the bondage of sin, however, God can divinely intervene.

If you desire to be set free, my brother and sister, you do not have to be bundled with the same kind you used to gravitate toward. If you give your life completely to Jesus Christ, without reservations or restrictions, you will be delivered to serve Him.

In this last hour, you will witness a bundling together of wickedness. You are going to see it on your job and in your community. Even in the Church, you are going to see a separating and clustering together of certain types of people.

Avoid getting into isolated groups because you will miss the move of God. Shun cliques because they are the bundles. Endeavor to stay in the mainstream of the move of God.

> *Endeavor to stay in the*
> *mainstream move of God.*

Keep involved where God has called you to serve. Don't compromise your position with God by getting involved with others of a different spirit. Don't try to fit into any one little group. Stay in the mainstream of what God has for you.

I'm so glad I'm not in any of the bundles that are to be burned. Although I may sometimes feel alienated from those who choose not to walk with God, He has assured me through His Word and by His Spirit that He will never leave me nor forsake me.

Don't allow the enemy to convince you that no one understands you and that you don't have any true friends. God may be sparing you from getting involved in certain cliques because they are being gathered together in bundles to be burned. It is better to be lonely and be gathered in the righteousness of God in Christ Jesus than to have fellowship with the unfruitful works of darkness.

You may occasionally experience trials of loneliness because you have decided to follow

Christ regardless of the cost or sacrifice. How-ever, you must begin to rejoice in such tribulation because "all things work together for good to them that love God, to them who are the called according to His purpose" (Rom. 8:28). Just be patient, and God will bring the right fellowship to you at the right time.

> *It's better to gather in righteousness than fellowship with darkness.*

God's Divine Separation

God's will is that we, as His people, be separated unto Him for His purpose. As believers, we should endeavor to pursue that sanctification at any cost.

How are we sanctified? By God's Spirit, through His Word, and by the one-time blood offering of Christ, He "hath perfected for ever them that are sanctified" (Heb. 10:14). Theologically, this is called a positional truth, a truth God has ordained and provided for His chosen people, regardless of whether we partake of it or not.

How can we realistically and practically appropriate the truth of sanctification in our lives? How do we transform in our lives this positional truth into experiential truth? How do we cause His will in Heaven to become a tangible reality in our lives here on earth?

What is sanctification? According to Vine's Expository Dictionary of Biblical Words, the Greek word for sanctification, *hagiasmos*, means "the separation of the believer from evil things and ways."

> *For this is the will of God, even your sanctification, that ye should abstain from fornication: that every one of you should know how to possess his vessel in sanctification and honour; not in the lust of concupiscence, even as the Gentiles which know not God... For God hath not called us unto uncleanness, but unto holiness* (1 Thessalonians 4:3-5,7).

The Word of God clearly declares it is His will that we, as sons of God, be separated unto Him from the immoral acts of the world and that we abstain from the lusts of the flesh. The Scripture goes on to imply that we, as born-again Christians, should know how to do this. Just because we are born again does not mean that we experience sanctification automatically.

Holiness, which actually comes from *hagiasmos*, the same Greek word for sanctification, is a Christian character trait developed by the continual application of God's Word, and the constant yielding to His Holy Spirit. Being holy does not happen involuntarily; it takes effort on our part.

Vine's Expository Dictionary explains that sanctification is not vicarious. In other words, it is not something that happens automatically, just because a person is born again:

> It [sanctification] cannot be transferred or imputed; it is an individual possession, built up, little by little, as the result of obedience to the Word of God and following the example of Christ in the power of the Holy Spirit (see Matt. 11:29; John 13:15; Eph. 4:20; Phil. 2:5).

How does this *"power"* work in our lives?

In John 1:12-13, God's Word explains "that as many as received Him [Jesus], to them gave He power to become the sons of God, even to them that believe on His name: which were born, not of blood, nor of the will of the flesh, nor of the will of man, but of the will of God."

The word *power* in this passage is not the word we have come to know as *dunamis*, which comes from the same English root word we use for dynamite. Biblically, *dunamis* signifies power that is to be used for the purpose of witnessing the gospel. (See Acts 1:8.)

The word *power*, as utilized in John 1:12, is the word, *exousia*, which means the right to exercise (delegated) authority and/or the right to act on another's behalf or authority.

In simpler terms, Scripture teaches that receiving Christ as your personal Savior does not necessarily make you a son of God, but if you choose to receive Him, the power (authority) and right to do so is present.

Are You Willing?

Just being saved does not make you a son of God, as the apostle Paul explained to the Roman Christians:

For if ye live after the flesh, ye shall die: but if ye through the Spirit do mortify the deeds of the body, ye shall live. For as many as are led by the Spirit of God, they are the sons of God. For ye have not received the Spirit of bondage again unto fear; but ye have received the Spirit of adoption, whereby we cry, Abba, Father (Romans 8:13-15).

This passage clearly indicates that only those who are willing to be led by the Spirit actually realize and manifest the sonship of God: "For as many as are led by the Spirit of God, they are the sons of God" (Rom. 8:14). Sanctification is an act of our will, as well as a work of the grace of God through the Holy Spirit.

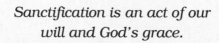

> *Sanctification is an act of our will and God's grace.*

Sanctification means living a holy life, in which the believer is separated from the world, and the influences of worldly people, by the Father through the Word and the Spirit. As we enter the era of end-time harvest, this is what Christ endeavors to do among His Body and His Church to sanctify us and set us apart from the world.

Why? Because, before there can be a fruitful harvest, there must first be a reaping, or separation of the tares from the wheat. Will you be separated unto God or bundled to burn? The choice is yours.

Just as there is a harvest of righteousness to be reaped by the children of promise, there is also a harvest of evil and unrighteousness to be reaped by the children of disobedience. May you know how to rightly discern between good and evil, the difference between spiritual night and day, and what's biblically right and wrong.

Thoughts and Reflections

_____

_____

_____

_____

_____

_____

_____

_____

_____

_____

_____

_____

_____

_____

_____

_____

_____

_____

_____

_____

Chapter 4
The Only Safe Place

The Only Safe Place

The Word of God calls Noah a *"preacher of righteousness"* (2 Pet. 2:5) who, "prepared an ark to the saving of his house; by the which he condemned the world, and became heir of the righteousness which is by faith" (Heb. 11:7).

During the 120 years that Noah worked on the ark, he brought his generation God's message of judgment. Over and over again, Noah preached that because of man's wickedness, God was going to send rain so hard and heavy and long that the earth would be deluged with water.

In those days, rain was an unknown phenomenon. The earth, enveloped with a protective canopy, enjoyed a tropical climate year round. Much like a terrarium, the earth's moisture was self-contained, making rain unnecessary.

The people mocked and criticized Noah, calling him a fool for his supposed attempt to save his family and himself from a flood, an idea completely foreign to them. It seemed ludicrous to think that the entire earth could be completely covered with water.

In spite of the ridicule from his peers, Noah preached a controversial, unbelievable, and unpopular message unlike the widely accepted, lukewarm, and nonconfrontational preaching of today. Noah's message was rejected because he preached righteousness in the midst of a wicked and perverse generation. In fact, the only converts he won to God were those of his own household.

What were the days of Noah like? Jesus described them this way:

They did eat, they drank, they married wives, they were given in marriage, until the day that [Noah] *entered into the ark,*

*and the flood came, and destroyed them
all* (Luke 17:27).

The people acted as if life, as they knew it,
would go on forever without interruption. Until
the day that Noah entered the ark, the people
were neither convinced nor moved by the reality
of the impending and inevitable flood. Why were
they so skeptical? Because, like the children of
Israel in the wilderness, their evil hearts were
full of unbelief and that led to their destruction.

In the end, Noah's persistence, labor, and
admonition to his family paid off, and they along
with two of every animal on the face of the earth
were able to escape the doom and destruction
of the flood God had promised 120 years before.

After the waters receded, God made a covenant
with Noah that He would never again destroy
the earth and its inhabitants by way of a flood.
Today, when it rains, God places a rainbow in
the sky to remind all mankind of His promise to
Noah over 5,000 years ago.

The Ark of Safety

God said, the next time He destroys the
earth because of the wickedness of man, it will
not be with water but with fire. We have already
discussed how God is preparing to gather the

servants of sin and wickedness in bundles to be burned. Will anyone be safe from God's final judgment of fire?

The only ark and place of safety today is to be baptized by the Spirit of the living God into the Body of Christ, which is represented by the living organism called the Church.

> *The ark of safety is the Spirit of the living God.*

The apostle Paul explained what it means to be *"baptized into one body"*:

> *For by one Spirit are we all baptized into one body, whether we be Jews or Gentiles, whether we be bond or free; and have been all made to drink into one Spirit* (1 Corinthians 12:13).

> *There is one body, and one Spirit, even as ye are called in one hope of your calling; one Lord, one faith, one baptism, one God and Father of all, who is above all, and through all, and in you all* (Ephesians 4:4-6).

Local churches function as the arms and legs of the Body of believers, the Church of Jesus Christ.

Some people, however, are reluctant to become members of churches and for valid reasons. In many cases, churches have failed to meet the spiritual needs of the people.

People come to church hurting, desperate, and needing a touch from God, only to find no comfort, no help, and no word from the Lord. They meet insensitive people, who are only concerned about their own needs and feelings, and care little about the needs of the lost.

Other seekers briefly find some solace within the sanctum of the four walls of the church. Over the course of time, however, they find themselves taken advantage of and exploited by so-called "church leadership." As a result, they become disillusioned and discouraged from even coming to the house of God.

Then, there are the zealous, new Christians who eagerly desire to serve the Lord, but who, unfortunately, are shunned and hurt by lukewarm church members, jealous of the new members' zeal. Once again, the church fails to meet the needs of those who are looking to them for spiritual guidance and protection.

This, of course, is the plan of the devil, who knows the best way to win a battle is to divide and conquer. If satan can get individual saints isolated and outside the protective covering of a local fellowship of believers, he can convince them they are all alone and nobody cares.

When people are alone—without the help and encouragement of other like-minded believers—they are susceptible to satan's lies. As a result, they begin to think they might as well give up and throw in the towel because, after all, nobody cares anyway.

When people feel isolated, unfortunately, it is often sinners who appear to show more love, concern, and consideration than the hypocritical, pretentious, and condemning saints back at the church. Shame on us.

God's Haven for the Oppressed

As people of God, we must stop simply going through the motions of religious exercises. The reason for assembling together to fellowship and worship is not so we will have a nice place to go or an excuse to show off our latest outfit on Sunday mornings.

> *We must stop going through the motions of religious exercises.*

The Church is a living entity, a spiritual organism, where abundant life exists here on earth. The Body of Christ must be a present reminder of the hope we have for the hereafter, a place where people can go to escape hell and the wrath to come.

And I say also unto thee, That thou art Peter, and upon this rock I will build My church; and the gates of hell shall not prevail against it (Matthew 16:18).

The local church—not Alcoholics Anonymous or the local support group—should be the place where sinners can be freed from their addictions.

God wants to deliver the crack-head and the cocaine addict, without admitting them to a substance abuse center and without withdrawal. The purpose of the local church is to provide a haven where the alcoholic and drug addict can come to Jesus Christ, be set free, and get high on the new wine of the Holy Spirit.

Homosexuals should not be afraid to come out of the closet and come to church to be delivered by the blood of Jesus and the cleansing power of the Holy Spirit. The Church must welcome homosexuals without making them feel they are going to be condemned or persecuted by stiff-necked, two-faced, holier-than-thou, so-called Christians.

If homosexuals, lesbians, fornicators, adulterers, child abusers, molestation victims, rape victims, or rapists can't get set free and delivered in the Church of Almighty God, where else can they be set free? The Church is not a social club; it's a life raft thrown out to the sinking man or woman, boy or girl, who is overcome by sin and dying because of it.

The message of the Church is: Sinner, you don't have to drown in your sins if you don't want to. God's arm is not too short to reach out and save you. His ears are open to hear your cry for help.

God, in His Word, makes it clear that He is ready and willing to rescue the lost and dying.

Behold, the Lord's hand is not short-ened, that it cannot save; neither His ear heavy, that it cannot hear (Isaiah 59:1).

Not only must we convey this message to those who are floundering in their sins, but we need to realize that "rescuing the perishing" is God's purpose for the Church.

Preoccupied Harvesters

Jesus, in discussing the endtimes with the disciples, said that the coming harvest of souls into the kingdom of God would signify the end of this present world order.

When asked to explain the parable of the tares, Jesus responded:

> *...The harvest is the end of the world; and the reapers are the angels. As therefore the tares are gathered and burned in the fire; so shall it be in the end of this world* (Matthew 13:39-40).

Christ's relating of the harvest to the so-called "end of this world" has caused some Christians to erroneously assume that the endtime reaping will not take place in our lifetime. As a result, many people in the Church are complacent and insensitive in their desire to see the lost saved.

All around the world, revival is occurring, but the American Church seems to be consumed with the "me, myself, and I" attitude. Likewise, we have become lackadaisical in our attempt to live holy lives, ignoring the reality that our Redeemer—as well as our redemption—draws near.

The Body of Christ has become preoccupied with financial prosperity, material well-being, and attempting to satisfy our own spiritual overindulgence. As a result, we have neglected the work and will of God in evangelizing even those within our own community.

When Jesus was confronted with the same dilemma of choosing between providing for His own personal physical needs or meeting the spiritual needs of others, His response was, "My meat is to do the will of Him that sent Me, and to finish His work" (John 4:34).

Instead of believing God for the salvation of family, friends, and communities, many are preoccupied with using their faith solely for the purpose of believing God for houses, cars, and vacations. They quote, "Faith is the substance of things hoped for, the evidence of things not seen" (Heb. 11:1).

"Things" have come to mean the material and temporal possessions of this world, rather than the eternal "things" of that "better country" (Heb. 11:16) that the patriarchs of old desired. Instead of setting our affections and sights on things above, realizing that only what we do for Christ will last for eternity, we live contrary to those men and women of faith spoken about in Hebrews chapter eleven.

This is not to imply that financial and material prosperity is sinful or wrong in and of itself. However, we are admonished to seek the kingdom of God first and foremost, and inevitably all these other things will be added to us. (see Matt. 6:33.) In fact, we don't necessarily have to believe God for those earthly and material things; they will, without asking, be given to us, as we seek His kingdom.

Saying "Yes" to God

The harvest is near. In fact, the time has come when the Lord is gathering His people together.

Jesus said that in the last days of earth the householder will gather the children of the kingdom together. When this happens, the children of God will be vividly distinct from the people of this world. "Then shall the righteous shine forth as the sun in the kingdom of their Father..." (Matt. 13:43).

God declares, "I'm gathering My people into the barn. I'm going to put them where the enemy can't get to them. I'm going to put them in a place of safety. I'm going to give them a place of refuge." (See Matthew 13:30.)

Regardless of all the violence and destruction presently taking place in this world, God's people are assured of a safe place in the loving hands of Jesus. Speaking of His followers, Jesus said, "They shall never perish, neither shall any man pluck them out of My hand" (John 10:28).

God's people are assured of safety in Jesus' loving hands.

A time comes in every believer's life when he or she decides not to deviate from the straight and narrow path. As a believer, you know you have gone too far with God to turn around and follow the devil. That doesn't mean you won't be tempted to sin or that your trials and tribulations will end.

Serving the Lord is not always easy or popular. Folks may laugh at you on your job, mocking and making fun of your faith. But once you decide that there's no turning back, something in your heart rises up and says "no" to the devil and "yes" to the Lord.

The time comes when you make up your mind that you're going to praise God, even in the midst of the most trying and difficult situations. Drugs are all around, but you will stand firm. Guns are in the streets, but you refuse to be afraid. People robbing, stealing, and killing, but you are determined to praise the Lord, in spite of the circumstances.

As for myself, I must praise Him. Regardless of how rough the road appears to be, I have determined I am going to rejoice and worship and praise the Lord with my whole heart. No matter how strong the battles may rage, with Christ I can do all things; for it is He who strengthens me. (See Philippians 4:13.) Jesus is my place of refuge.

What Is God's Agenda?

If we are seeking God's kingdom, then we want Him to rule on the earth. The rule of God is His will, and it is not God's will that any should be lost, but that all should be saved. The salvation of the lost is primary on God's agenda.

Is that your top priority in life?

Many in the Church are living only for today rather than storing up treasures for eternity. Our motto has become a hedonistic obsession that says: Live for today, for tomorrow you die.

In Jesus' parable of the rich fool, He wanted to make the point that "a man's life consisteth not in the abundance of the things which he possesseth" (Luke 12:15).

Americans have taken what Jesus referred to as "abundant life" (John 10:10) and misinterpreted it as the accumulation of monetary and material wealth. As a result, our attitude has become that of the fool who says, "Chill out, eat, drink, and be merry!"

God's response to this attitude is, "Thou fool, this night thy soul shall be required of thee: then whose shall those things be, which thou hast provided? So is he that layeth up treasure for himself, and is not rich toward God" (Luke 12:20-21).

According to Deuteronomy 8:18, God has given us "power to get wealth" so that His covenant may be established with His people. Salvation, being born-again, is the initiation of that covenant relationship.

If we really care about the poor and those less fortunate, we need to get with God's agenda. The best way to help them out of their poverty and despair is to guide them into this covenant relationship with the God of the universe.

On the other hand, those of us who have experienced the blessings of God's covenant must not allow our wealth to become the focus of our lives. We must keep our hearts and minds fixed on God's agenda—saving the lost.

> *We must keep our hearts and minds fixed on God's agenda.*

Sometimes, however, we get sidetracked. Our attitude about the lost implies that we believe "harvest time" will take place in the far, distant future. As a result, it is not a present reality. Such thinking is contrary to the teaching of Jesus, who said:

> *Say not ye, There are four months, and then cometh harvest? behold, I say unto you, Lift up your eyes and look on the fields; for they are white already to harvest. And he that reapeth receiveth wages, and gathereth fruit unto life eternal...* (John 4:35-36).

All the signs of the times indicate, according to the end-time teachings of Jesus, we are near the climax of this present world order and the culmination of biblical prophecies relating to the return of Christ. We should "walk circumspectly, not as fools," but as wise men and women of God, "redeeming the time" because the days in which we live are evil and getting worse. "Wherefore be not unwise, but understanding what the will of the Lord is " (Eph. 5:15-17).

How do you know if you are wise? The Bible says "he that winneth souls is wise" (Prov. 11:30).

What is the will of the Lord? It is not God's will that any man be lost, but He wants all people "to be saved, and to come unto the knowledge of the truth" (1 Tim. 2:4).

God's objective is clear. The dilemma presently confronting us in light of the wickedness in the world is not that men do not seek to know God. The problem is: the Church has a tremendous shortage of sold-out, unselfish Christians committed to the *salvation* and *discipleship* of the lost.

Christian men and women of God must be willing to go into the highways of greed-ridden corporate America and the byways of our sin-ravaged inner cities and compel men, women, and children to come to the Lord.

"The harvest truly is great, but the labourers are few: pray ye therefore the Lord of the harvest, that He would send forth labourers into

His harvest" (Luke 10:2). May that be our most earnest prayer.

Rising to the Occasion

Why is there such an attack on Christians? Why is there so much controversy and slander going on in the organized Church, especially now, when the world is in such need of what the true Church of God and His Christ have to offer?

The devil knows that the Church is the most authentic representation of God and His will on earth. Without a spiritually healthy, unified Body of believers, God cannot conduct His affairs on earth in relation to mankind. The devil knows he is no match for God; therefore, in order to wreak his havoc against mankind, he must first try to subdue and defeat the Church, the Body of Christ, in whatever manner and degree he can.

In addition to being a haven for the oppressed, the Church, in many ways, is like a hospital for saints wounded on the battlefield of spiritual warfare. By imparting truth and a fresh anointing of the Holy Spirit, the Church functions as a recuperation center for those who have become weary.

The Church is also a training and assignment base for warriors and ambassadors of Christ. As Jesus' army on earth, the Church upholds the defense against satan and all the works of darkness.

The Bible says that, in these last days, the Church will make known to the principalities and powers in heavenly places "the manifold wisdom of God, according to the eternal purpose which He purposed in Christ Jesus our Lord" (Eph. 3:10-11).

As the Church fulfills her God-ordained purpose here on earth, she will reveal the mystery of God's desire to redeem mankind from the impending destruction that satan hopes to bring upon it. Through the example and leadership of the Church, God seeks to reveal His intent to administer in the affairs of mankind. In essence, the Church on earth is the beginning of "the kingdoms of this world" becoming "the kingdoms of our Lord, and of His Christ..." (Rev. 11:15).

As the pillar of truth, the Church must now rise to the occasion and obey the mandate assigned to her. We must accept the responsibility to be God's battle ax and weapon of warfare to be used in redeeming this wicked world back to its rightful Lord—Jesus Christ.

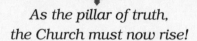

As the pillar of truth,
the Church must now rise!

Only the Church has the God-given power and right to act and speak to this world on God's behalf. But we must never forget that to whom much is given, much is required. (see Luke 12:48.)

The Church's Finest Hour

We are now quickly approaching the day of the Second Coming of the Lord Jesus Christ. How do we know?

> *Likewise also as it was in the days of Lot; they did eat, they drank, they bought, they sold, they planted, they builded.... Even thus shall it be in the day when the Son of man is revealed* (Luke 17:28,30).

Many preachers are not preparing the Church for the return of Christ. Instead, they are preoccupied with teaching us how to think and grow rich in this world. Rather than inspiring the Body of Christ to win souls to the kingdom of God and lay up eternal treasures in Heaven, we are taught how to build our own personal kingdoms here on earth.

We need men and women of God who will intercede for the lost souls of our families and communities. We need intercessors who will weep between the altar and the porch of the house of God, so that it will once again become a house of prayer, and no longer a den of wolves and a house of thieves. (See Matthew 21:13.)

The Church desperately needs righteous men and women of God who will lift up their voices like a trumpet and cry aloud. The Church needs "preachers of righteousness" (2 Pet. 2:5) who are not afraid to proclaim to the Body of Christ their sins and reveal their transgressions.

A great harvest of souls waits to be won to Christ. Men, women, boys, and girls are discouraged and discontent with the world's status quo. They are looking for answers to the problematic and disastrous conditions that plague our society. People are hurting and seeking relief from the pain and heartache of this wicked and perverse generation.

◆

> *A great harvest of souls waits to be won to Christ.*

The people of the world are searching for something or someone they can believe in, trust in, and depend on to give them hope and courage to face another tomorrow in this cruel and cold world. As born-again children of God and citizens of the kingdom of the Lord Jesus Christ, we have the answers to the world's problems, and know the Someone in Whom the lost can believe to fulfill every void and save them from the destruction to come.

It is up to us to tell them, "Whosoever shall call upon the name of the Lord shall be saved" (Rom. 10:13).

The apostle Paul asked the Roman Christians:

How then shall they call on Him in whom they have not believed? and how shall they believe in Him of whom they have not heard? and how shall they hear without a preacher? And how shall they preach, except they be sent? as it is written, How beautiful are the feet of them that preach the gospel of peace, and bring glad tidings of good things! (Romans 10:14-15).

In this hour, as it was in the days of Noah, we desperately need "preachers of righteousness."

Today is "harvest time," and the Church must go forth and reap souls for the kingdom of God. Other believers have gone before us and planted seeds of righteousness, and many have continued to water the hearts of men with the water of the Word of God. Now it is this generation's responsibility and obligation to go forth and reap the harvest of those who have faithfully labored before us.

This is the Church's finest hour. Although we have a great challenge ahead of us, God has empowered us to successfully complete the assignment. And what an assignment it is!

Thoughts and Reflections

Chapter 5
Are You Ready?

Are You Ready?

I n biblical times, before the wheat was gathered into a barn and used to make flour, it had to go through a process referred to as "threshing." Threshing is similar to the way we sift flour or corn meal for baking needs today.

When the wheat crop was gathered, certain parts were not suitable for human consumption. Only the grains on the end of the plant were useful for making flour. The fruitful portion of the wheat plant was separated using the threshing process.

This was done by spreading the gathered wheat stalks on a flat, open space or surface called a threshing floor. These floors were usually located on hillsides or mountaintops where strong winds frequently blew. The dried stalks of wheat were then crushed by using heavy objects or weighted sleds driven by oxen back and forth over the wheat-covered floors (see 1 Chron. 21:20-23).

John the Baptist used the threshing of wheat to illustrate God's impending judgment.

> *I indeed baptize you with water unto repentance: but He that cometh after me is mightier than I, whose shoes I am not worthy to bear: He shall baptize you with the Holy Ghost, and with fire: whose fan is in His hand, and He will thoroughly purge His floor, and gather His wheat into the garner; but He will burn up the chaff with unquenchable fire* (Matthew 3:11-12).

On the day of judgment, God will "gather the wheat"—those who have been transformed by the Spirit and conformed into the image of Christ. At the same time, those who have not been conformed to the image of Christ —"the chaff"— will be burned with unquenchable fire.

The Work of the Holy Spirit

As Christians, we have chaff in our lives—flaws and unrighteous elements of our character that are not conducive to a holy walk with the Lord. Some of us are like the religious leaders who came to hear John the Baptist:

> *But when he saw many of the Pharisees and Sadducees come to his baptism, he said unto them, O generation of vipers, who hath warned you to flee from the wrath to come? Bring forth therefore fruits meet for repentance* (Matthew 3:7-8).

In other words, God demands more than lip service. The outward displays of piety by these religious leaders were insufficient to warrant the forgiveness of their sins. They had a form of religious worship, but in their hearts they failed to submit themselves sincerely to the will of Almighty God.

> *God demands more than life service.*

The Pharisees and Sadducees brought their religious words and deeds, but like the undesirable and unproductive wheat chaff, their fruit was not acceptable in the sight of God. They had a "form of godliness" but denied the power thereof (2 Tim. 3:5).

Anything in our lives that does not conform to the image of Christ must be dealt with and purged by the Holy Spirit, who acts like a refiner to cleanse and mold us into the image of Christ.

When we are born again, our spirit man is instantly renewed in newness of life by the Spirit of God. Our souls, as well as our physical bodies, however, are yet to be completely redeemed.

Our bodies will be redeemed either when we die or when Jesus returns for His Church. The full salvation of our souls is a continued work of sanctification by the Holy Spirit that lasts as long as we live in these mortal bodies.

> *If the Spirit of Him that raised up Jesus from the dead dwell in you, He that raised up Christ from the dead shall also quicken your mortal bodies by His Spirit that dwelleth in you. Therefore, brethren, we are debtors, not to the flesh, to live after the flesh. For if ye live after the flesh, ye shall die: but if ye through the Spirit do mortify the deeds of the body, ye shall live* (Romans 8:11-13).

The Spirit does the work of threshing in our mortal bodies. While the Spirit brings death to our unrighteous deeds, it will at the same time give life to our mortal bodies.

The Spirit does the work of threshing in our mortal bodies.

Wheat or Tares?

All wheat is not as fruitful as other wheat. Some varieties of wheat are not as productive as others. Some wheat is weak, but it is still wheat. Like any other crop, wheat may be adversely affected by the presence of weeds, insects, or weather conditions that can destroy the life of an otherwise healthy and fruitful plant.

Many times, because we are unable to distinguish the consecrating, sanctifying, and purifying work of the Holy Spirit in a particular believer's life, we are too quick to label a person a "tare" when that individual very well may be weak wheat.

Why is that? Because of the similarity between the two, as the householder in Jesus' parable emphasized:

...The servants said unto him, Wilt thou then that we go and gather them [the tares] up? But he said, Nay; lest while ye gather up the tares, ye root up also the wheat with them. Let both grow together until the harvest (Matthew 13:28-30a).

The farmer must wait until the crops are full-grown before attempting to separate the tares from the wheat. In the infant and adolescent stages, wheat appears very similar to tares.

Likewise, when Christians are newly converted and young in the faith, they act very much like children of the world. It is quite normal and expected for children to behave like children.

God does not expect us always to act like children, tossed to and fro by every wind of doctrine. (see Eph. 4:14.) This is precisely why "as newborn babes," we are admonished in Scripture, to "desire the sincere milk of the word, that [we] may grow thereby" (1 Pet. 2:2). As we mature, we are able to lay aside "all malice, and all guile, and hypocrisies, and envies, and all evil speakings" (1 Pet. 2:1).

The apostle Paul said, "When I was child, I spake as a child, I understood as a child, I thought as a child: but when I became a man,

I put away childish things" (1 Cor. 13:11). It is time for some Christians to grow up and stop gossiping, complaining, and ridiculing one another.

Thankfully, we are not alone in our growth process because "the Spirit also helpeth our infirmities" (Rom. 8:26). The Spirit of the Almighty God enables us to overcome the strongholds in our lives, empowering us to stand in the face of great temptation from the evil one.

Revealed by Fire

After the wheat has been harvested and sifted, the chaff and other unproductive portions of the wheat plant must be destroyed. This is usually done by fire. The Christian life must go through the same process.

God demands that we, as children of God, go on to maturity. This usually requires a season of purification in which the Lord tests the motives of our hearts and burns out the impurities.

Every man's work shall be made manifest: for the day shall declare it, because it shall be revealed by fire; and the fire shall try every man's work of what sort it is (1 Corinthians 3:13).

At some point, God will no longer wink at the sin in our lives. We must grow from being vessels of dishonor to become vessels of honor—no longer vessels of wood and clay, but vessels of gold, available for the Master's use. The apostle Paul explained it this way:

> *In a great house there are not only vessels of gold and of silver, but also of wood and of earth; and some to honour, and some to dishonour. If a man therefore purge himself from these, he shall be a vessel unto honour, sanctified, and meet for the master's use, and prepared unto every good work* (2 Timothy 2:20-21).

In every person's life there are certain areas that are contrary to the will of God. No matter how hard you try in your own strength to change these areas of weakness, they remain the same.

You may not commit any open and blatant sins, but what about the condition of your heart? The Bible declares that God does not look upon the outward appearance of men, but on the heart—which is "deceitful above all things, and desperately wicked: who can know it?" (Jer. 17:9).

> *God doesn't look upon
> the outward appearance,
> but on the heart.*

You may not have a problem with fornication, drinking, lying, stealing, or drug addiction; but is your heart filled with hate, malice, pride, or self-ish ambition? Are you holding unforgiveness toward anyone? Do you gossip and backbite? If these strongholds are in your heart, your heart is just as wicked and deceitful as the fornicator, adulterer, thief, or murderer.

As we draw nearer to the time of Christ's return, the end of the harvest is imminent. Don't continue to live in sin or constantly worry about the things of this world. If you do, you may fail to be part of this final harvest.

John the Baptist gave this warning to those whose lives were not bearing the kind of spiritual fruit that God requires:

And now also the ax is laid unto the root of the trees: therefore every tree which bringeth not forth good fruit is hewn down, and cast into the fire (Matthew 3:10).

Now is the time to get right with God—before it is too late. God help you if you miss the harvest.

Nothing but the Blood of Jesus

In the Old Testament, the blood of bulls and goats was only effective to sanctify "to the purifying of the flesh" (Heb. 9:13). It could not purge man's conscience—the "hidden man of the heart" (1 Peter 3:4)—from dead works to serve freely, without guilt, the living God. The perfect blood of Jesus, however, was able "through the eternal Spirit" (Heb. 9:14), to wash and cleanse the inward man, the heart (see Heb. 9:11-14).

It is the consecrating work of the Holy Spirit that cleanses us from impure affections and desires. That is why John the Baptist told the people that the One who was to come after him would baptize, not with water, but "with the Holy Ghost, and with fire" (Matt. 3:11).

John knew that neither the Law nor the baptism of repentance was able to change the conditions of the heart. Regardless of the Jews' ability to keep the Law of Moses, they were plagued with character flaws such as pride, vanity, hatred, selfish ambition, unforgiveness, and many other evil conditions of the heart.

For what the Law could not do, in that it was weakened by the flesh, the Spirit was able to do by the changing of the heart. The Law brought death, but the Spirit brought life.

*For the law of the Spirit of life in Christ
Jesus hath made me free from the law of
sin and death. For what the law could
not do, in that it was weak through the
flesh, God sending His own Son in the
likeness of sinful flesh, and for sin, condemned sin in the flesh: that the
righteousness of the law might be fulfilled
in us, who walk not after the flesh, but
after the Spirit* (Romans 8:2-4).

It is the Spirit that empowers our soul to
choose to do right according to God's will.

Dirty Danny's Day of Salvation

John the Baptist said that the One who
was to come after him would not baptize with
water, but with the Holy Ghost and with fire—
and that fire is a cleansing fire, a purging fire,
a purifying fire.

That is what the Dirty Dannys of this world
need in order to be gathered into bundles of
righteousness—fire, Holy Ghost fire.

Today, people are getting saved that no one
ever thought would come to the Lord. Slick Sally
and Dirty Danny, who spent their lives in the
clubs, drinking and carousing and doing every

117

unholy and unlawful thing, are coming under conviction in this last hour of earth's time clock.

> *People are getting saved that no one thought would come to God.*

Suddenly, old Dirty Danny says one day, "I'm going to church."

When he gets there, he cries his heart out at the altar, weeping and earnestly repenting of his sin before God.

"I never thought I would ever see Dirty Danny in church," you say to your fellow pew-warmer.

What you did not know is that Dirty Danny belonged to God all along. Even when he was drinking liquor and running around in the street, he was one of God's chosen. Danny just didn't know it yet.

God had an appointed time for Dirty Danny's salvation. Before the foundations of the earth were laid, God, by His foreknowledge and predestined will, set a specific time and particular place in destiny when He would reach down, pull Dirty Danny out of the muck and mire, and wash him in the cleansing blood of the Lord Jesus Christ. Not only will the heavenly Father cleanse Dirty Danny with the blood of Jesus, God will also sanctify Danny by His Spirit.

God is saving the Dirty Dannys of this world and bringing them into the church because God is gathering His people together. God is bringing in the last of the crop of saints. The final gleaning of wheat from the harvest is coming in now.

You don't have time to say, "Tomorrow I'll get busy for God." You don't have time to think about doing it later.

Jesus told His disciples, "Look! The harvest is ripe right now!"

...Look on the fields; for they are white already to harvest. And he that reapeth receiveth wages, and gathereth fruit unto life eternal... (John 4:35-36).

People are not only ready to be saved, but there are plenty of them. Jesus said, "The harvest truly is great..." (Luke 10:2).

The fields that Jesus said are "white" with wheat and ready for harvest represent men and women whose hearts are eager to respond

119

to the gospel message of salvation. Are you ready for them?

The Time of Ingathering

As the earth remains there will always be seedtime and harvest, cold and heat, summer and winter, and day and night will never cease (see Genesis 8:22.)

In seedtime and harvest there is, and always will be, a season to plant seed and a time to reap—to harvest what has been planted.

To every thing there is a season, and a time to every purpose under the heaven: A time to be born, and a time to die; a time to plant, and a time to pluck up that which is planted (Ecclesiastes 3:1-2).

These established spiritual and physical laws are fixed, regardless of man's attempt and persistence to manipulate and alter the physical and natural elements of the earth. As long as the earth exists, these laws will never cease.

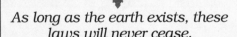

As long as the earth exists, these laws will never cease.

The harvest season in ancient Israel was celebrated as the time of year when the grain crops came to full maturity and were ready to be gathered. Harvest represents the time of fulfillment.

Another name for the Feast of Pentecost is the Feast of Harvest or "Feast of Ingathering" (Exod. 23:16). This seasonal celebration marked the culmination of the grain harvest and lasted for weeks. It was a time of great excitement and joyful thanksgiving to God, acknowledging that He was the source of their total supply—their all-sufficiency.

It was this celebration of the "Feast of Ingathering" that was taking place on the day we Christians refer to as the "day of Pentecost"— when the Holy Spirit was poured out on Jesus' disciples. This day is significant because it marks the time when the crop of souls started coming into the kingdom of God.

> *And when the day of Pentecost was fully come, they were all with one accord in one place. And suddenly there came a sound from heaven as of a rushing mighty wind, and it filled all the house where they were sitting. And there appeared unto them cloven tongues like as of fire, and it sat upon each of them. And they were all filled with the Holy Ghost, and began to speak with other*

tongues, as the Spirit gave them utter-
ance (Acts 2:1-4).

Peter was the first farmer to get out into
the field. When this apostle preached the
gospel on the day of Pentecost, 3,000 grains of
wheat (souls) were harvested. Leaving behind a
life of hopelessness and religious activity, they
were gathered into a personal relationship
with God through the blood and redemptive
work of the Lord Jesus Christ.

Until Jesus comes back, we as Christians
are to continually harvest souls from out of the
field of worldly darkness and despair.

The time of harvest has come. It's the time of
the ingathering.

Gathered From All Nations

Today in this time of spiritual harvest the
Spirit of God is preparing His people to be gathered into the heavenly barn. We are getting
ready to leave this world.

And then shall appear the sign of the Son
of man in heaven: and then shall all the
tribes of the earth mourn, and they shall
see the Son of man coming in the clouds
of heaven with power and great glory.

And He shall send his angels with a great sound of a trumpet, and they shall gather together his elect from the four winds, from one end of heaven to the other (Matthew 24:30-31).

When you see people coming to God from every nation and every tongue and every kindred, it is a sign that God is gathering His people.

The Holy Spirit told me, "The reason you're going to see a gathering of nations is because Jesus is soon to come."

"What do You mean, Lord?" I asked. "I thought the day of Pentecost was the ingathering."

He answered, "When Peter preached the gospel on that day, devout men came from every nation under Heaven: men of Judea, Samaria, and the regions round about; men from Medes, Mesopotamia, Cappadocia, Asia; men of Egypt, Libya, Cyrene, and strangers of Rome, Jews, Cretes and Arabians; men from the uttermost parts of the earth." (See Acts 2:5-11.)

The Lord said, "They did not come saying, 'I am from Judea, and you are from Samaria; we, therefore, can't get along together.' They all came under the same gospel and began to worship in one accord the One and true living God. There were no divisions among them. They all represented wheat. Black wheat, white wheat, red wheat, yellow wheat, and all the variations in between. The common denominator was that they were all wheat—all citizens of the kingdom of God."

God is sending out a call to His elect, and we are coming in out of every nation, every tongue, and every kindred.

God spoke to my heart and said, "I set a call into the earth. It is not only for black folks; it's not only for white people, or only for red or yellow races. It's for saved folks, and those who want to be saved."

God's chosen ones are coming out of every nation because it is harvest time.

In the past, we have seen moves of God that were carried out by men in the flesh. This time when we hear the Spirit call, we are going to see every nation coming to Christ and saying, "I heard it! I heard it! I was praying, and God spoke to me. I want to be saved!"

God is going to move across the world the way His Spirit did on the day of Pentecost 2,000 years ago. God is going to gather His people from every nation.

The world cannot get mankind together. None of their programs, none of their laws, none of their legislation, none of their marches have brought us together as one. Nothing but the blood of Jesus can bring together all men from every nation, tongue, and kindred. And now is the time! It is the time of the great ingathering of God's elect.

> *Nothing but the blood of Jesus can bring mankind together.*

It's harvest time. Will you be ready?

Thoughts and Reflections

◆ _____

_____

_____

_____

_____

_____

_____

_____

_____

_____

_____

_____

_____

_____

_____

_____

_____

_____

_____

_____

_____

_____

_____

_____

_____

_____

_____

_____

_____

_____

_____

_____

_____

_____

_____

_____

_____

_____

_____◆

Bonus Material

Chapter 1

Woman, Thou Art Loosed
Infirmed Woman

A nd, *behold, there was a woman which had a spirit of infirmity eighteen years, and was bowed together, and could in no wise lift up herself. And when Jesus saw her, He called her to Him, and said unto her, Woman, thou art loosed from thine infirmity* (Luke 13:11-12).

The Holy Spirit periodically lets us catch a glimpse of the personal testimony of one of the patients of the Divine Physician Himself. This

131

woman's dilemma is her own, but perhaps you will find some point of relativity between her case history and your own. She could be like someone you know or have known; she could even be like you.

There are three major characters in this story. These characters are the person, the problem, and the prescription. It is important to remember that for every person, there will be a problem. Even more importantly, for every problem, our God has a prescription!

Jesus' opening statement to the problem in this woman's life is not a recommendation for counseling—it is a challenging command! Often, much more is involved in maintaining deliverance than just discussing past trauma. Jesus did not counsel what should have been commanded. I am not, however, against seeking the counsel of godly men. On the contrary, the Scriptures say:

Blessed is the man that walketh not in the counsel of the ungodly, nor standeth in the way of sinners, nor sitteth in the seat of the scornful (Psalm 1:1).

Where no counsel is, the people fall: but in the multitude of counsellors there is safety (Proverbs 11:14).

What I want to make clear is that after you have analyzed the condition, after you have understood its origin, it will still take the authority of God's Word to put the past under your feet! This woman was suffering as a result of something that attacked her 18 years earlier. I wonder if you can relate to the long-range aftereffects of past pain? This kind of trauma is as fresh to the victim today as it was the day it occurred. Although the problem may be rooted in the past, the prescription is a present word from God! The Word is the same yesterday, today and forevermore! (See Hebrews 13:8.) That is to say, the word you are hearing today is able to heal your yesterday!

> *The word you are hearing today is able to heal your yesterday.*

Jesus said, "Woman, thou art loosed." He did not call her by name. He wasn't speaking to her just as a person. He spoke to her femininity. He spoke to the song in her. He spoke to the lace in her. Like a crumbling rose, Jesus spoke to what she could, and would, have been. I believe the Lord spoke to the twinkle that existed in her eye when she was a child; to the girlish glow that makeup can never seem to recapture. He spoke to her God-given uniqueness. He spoke to her gender.

Her problem didn't begin suddenly. It had existed in her life for 18 years. We are looking at a woman who had a personal war going on inside her. These struggles must have tainted many other areas of her life. The infirmity that attacked her life was physical. However, many women also wrestle with infirmities in emotional traumas. These infirmities can be just as challenging as a physical affliction. An emotional handicap can create dependency on many different levels. Relationships can become crutches. The infirmed woman then places such weight on people that it stresses healthy relationships. Many times such emotional handicaps will spawn a series of unhealthy relationships.

> *For thou hast had five husbands; and he whom thou now hast is not thy husband: in that saidst thou truly* (John 4:18).

Healing cannot come to a desperate person rummaging through other people's lives. One of the first things that a hurting person needs to do is break the habit of using other people as a narcotic to numb the dull aching of an inner void. The more you medicate the symptoms, the less chance you have of allowing God to heal you. The other destructive tendency that can exist with any abuse is the person must keep increasing the dosage. Avoid addictive, obsessive relationships. If you are becoming increasingly dependent upon anything other than God to create a sense of wholeness in your life, then you are abusing your relationships. Clinging to people is far different from loving them. It is not so much a statement of your love for them, as it is a crying out of your need for them. Like lust, it is intensely selfish. It is taking and not giving. Love is giving. God is love. God proved His love not by His need of us, but by His giving to us.

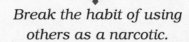

Break the habit of using others as a narcotic.

For God so loved the world, that He gave His only begotten Son, that whosoever believeth in Him should not perish, but have everlasting life (John 3:16).

The Scriptures plainly show that this infirmed woman had tried to lift herself. People who stand on the outside can easily criticize and assume that the infirmed woman lacks effort and fortitude. That is not always the case. Some situations in which we can find ourselves defy willpower. We feel unable to change. The Scriptures say that she "could in no wise lift up herself" (Luke 13:11.) That implies she had employed various means of self-ministry. Isn't it amazing how the same people who lift up countless others, often cannot lift themselves? This type of person may be a tower of faith and prayer for others, but impotent when it comes to his or her own limitations. That person may be the one others rely upon. Sometimes we esteem others more important than ourselves. We always become the martyr. It is wonderful to be self-sacrificing but watch out for self-disdain! If we don't apply some of the medicine that we use on others to strengthen ourselves, our patients will be healed and we will be dying.

I shall not die, but live, and declare the works of the Lord (Psalm 118:17).

Many things can engender disappointment and depression. In this woman's case, a spirit of infirmity had gripped her life. A spirit can manifest itself in many forms. For some it may be low self-esteem caused by child abuse, rape, wife abuse or divorce. I realize that these are natural problems, but they are rooted in spiritual ailments. One of the many damaging things that can affect us today is divorce, particularly among women, who often look forward to a happy relationship. Little girls grow up playing with Barbie and Ken dolls, dressing doll babies, and playing house. Young girls lie in bed reading romance novels, while little boys play ball and ride bicycles in the park. Whenever a woman is indoctrinated to think success is romance and then experiences the trauma of a failed relationship, she comes to a painful awakening. Divorce is not merely separating; it is the tearing apart of what was once joined together. Whenever something is torn, it does not heal easily. But Jesus can heal a broken or torn heart!

> *The Spirit of the Lord is upon Me, because He hath anointed Me to preach the gospel to the poor; He hath sent Me to heal the brokenhearted, to preach deliverance to the captives, and recovering of sight to the blind, to set at liberty them that are bruised* (Luke 4:18).

Approximately five out of ten marriages end in divorce. Those broken homes leave a trail of broken dreams, people, and children. Only the Master can heal these victims in the times in which we live. He can treat the long-term effects of this tragedy. One of the great healing balms of the Holy Spirit is forgiveness. To forgive is to break the link between you and your past. Sadly enough, many times the person hardest to forgive is the one in the mirror. Although they rage loudly about others, people secretly blame themselves for failed relationships. Regardless of whom you hold responsible, there is no healing in blame! When you begin to realize that your past does not necessarily dictate the outcome of your future, then you can release the hurt. It is impossible to inhale new air until you exhale the old. I pray that as you continue reading, God would give the grace of releasing where you have been, so you can receive what God has for you now. Exhale, then inhale; there is more for you.

Your past does not necessarily dictate the outcome of your future.

Perhaps one of the more serious indictments against our civilization is our flagrant disregard for the welfare of our children. Child abuse, regardless of whether it is physical, sexual, or emotional, is a terrible issue for an innocent mind to wrestle with. It is horrifying to think that little children who survive the peril of the streets, the public schools, and the aggravated society in which we live, come home to be abused in what should be a haven. Recent statistics suggest that three in five young girls in this country have been or will be sexually assaulted. If that many are reported, I shudder to think of those that never are reported but are covered with a shroud of secrecy.

If by chance you are a pastor, please realize that these figures are actually faces in your choir, committees, and so on. They reflect a growing amount of our congregational needs. Although this book focuses on women, many men also have been abused as children. I fear that God will judge us for our blatant disregard of this need in our messages, ministries and prayers. I even would suggest that our silence contributes to the shame and secrecy that satan attaches to these victimized persons. Whenever I think on these issues, I am reminded of what my mother used to say. I was forever coming home with a scratch or cut from schoolyard play. My mother would take the band-aid off, clean the wound and say, "Things that are covered don't heal well." Mother was right. Things that are covered do not heal well.

Perhaps Jesus was thinking on this order when He called the infirmed woman to come forward. It takes a lot of courage, even in church today, to receive ministry in sensitive areas. The Lord, though, is the kind of physician who can pour on the healing oil. Uncover your wounds in His presence and allow Him to gently heal the injuries. One woman found healing in the hem of His garment (see Mark 5:25-29). There is a balm in Gilead! (See Jeremiah 8:22.).

Even when the victim survives, there is still a casualty. It is the death of trust. Surely you realize that little girls tend to be trusting and unsuspicious. When those who should nurture and protect them violate that trust through illicit behavior, multiple scars result. It is like programming a computer with false information; you can get out of it only what has been programmed into it. When a man tells a little girl that his perverted acts are normal, she has no reason not to believe that what she is being taught is true. She is devoted to him, allowing him to fondle her or further misappropriate his actions toward her. Usually, the abuser is someone very close, with access to the child at vulnerable times. Fear is also a factor, as many children lay down with the cold taste of fear in their mouths. They believe the abuser could and would kill them for divulging his liberties against them. Some, as the victims of rape, feel physically powerless to wrestle with the assailant.

What kind of emotions might this kind of conduct bring out in the later life of this person? I am glad you asked. It would be easy for this kind of little girl to grow into a young lady who has difficulty trusting anyone! Maybe she learns to deal with the pain inside by getting attention in illicit ways. Drug rehabilitation centers and prisons are full of adults who were abused children needing attention.

Not every abused child takes such drastic steps. Often, their period of behavioral disorder dissipates with time. However, the abused child struggles with her own self-worth. She reasons, "How can I be valuable if the only way I could please my own father was to have sex with him?" This kind of childhood can affect how later relationships progress. Intimidated by intimacy, she struggles with trusting anyone. Insecurity and jealousy may be constant companions to this lady, who can't seem to grasp the idea that someone could love her. There are a variety of reactions as varied as there are individuals. Some avoid people who really care, being attracted to those who do not treat them well. Relating to abuse, they seem to sabotage good relationships and struggle for years in worthless ones. Still, others may be emotionally incapacitated to the degree that they need endless affirmation and affection just to maintain the courage to face ordinary days.

The pastor may tell this lady that God is her heavenly Father. That doesn't help, because the problem is her point of reference. We frame our references around our own experiences. If those experiences are distorted, our ability to comprehend spiritual truths can be off center. I know that may sound very negative for someone who is in that circumstance. What do you do when you have been poorly programmed by life's events? I've got good news! You can reprogram your mind through the Word of God.

> We frame our references around our own experiences.

Do not conform any longer to the pattern of this world, but be transformed by the renewing of your mind. Then you will be able to test and approve what God's will is—His good, pleasing and perfect will (Romans 12:2 NIV).

The Greek word metamorphôo is translated as "transformed" in this text. Literally, it means to change into another form! You can have a complete metamorphosis through the Word of God. It has been my experience as a pastor who does extensive counseling in my own ministry and abroad, that many abused people, women in particular, tend to flock to legalistic churches who see God primarily as a disciplinarian. Many times the concept of fatherhood for them is a harsh code of ethics. This type of domineering ministry may appeal to those who are performance-oriented. I understand that morality is important in Christianity; however, there is a great deal of difference between morality and legalism. It is important that God not be misrepresented. He is a balanced God, not an extremist.

The Word became flesh and made His dwelling among us. We have seen His glory, the glory of the One and Only, who came from the Father, full of grace and truth (John 1:14 NIV).

The glory of God is manifested only when there is a balance between grace and truth. Religion doesn't transform. Legalism doesn't transform. For the person who feels dirty, harsh rules could create a sense of self-righteousness. God doesn't have to punish you to heal you. Jesus has already prayed for you.

> *God doesn't have to punish you to heal you.*

Sanctify them through Thy truth: thy Word is truth (John 17:17).

Jesus simply shared grace and truth with that hurting woman. He said, "Woman, thou art loosed." Believe the Word of God and be free. Jesus our Lord was a great emancipator of the oppressed. It does not matter whether someone has been oppressed socially, sexually or racially; our Lord is an eliminator of distinctions.

> *There is neither Jew nor Greek* [racial],
> *there is neither bond nor free* [social],
> *there is neither male nor female* [sexual]:
> *for ye are all one in Christ Jesus* (Galatians 3:28).

I feel it is important to point out that this verse deals with unity and equality in regard to the covenant of salvation. That is to say, God is no respecter of persons. He tears down barriers that would promote prejudice and separation in the Body of Christ. Yet, it is important also to note that while there is no distinction in the manner in which we receive any of those groups, there should be an appreciation for the uniqueness of the groups individuality. There is a racial, social, and sexual uniqueness that we should not only accept, but also appreciate. It is cultural rape to teach other cultures or races that the only way to worship God is the way another race or culture worships. Unity should not come at the expense of uniqueness of expression. We

144

should also tolerate variance in social classes. It is wonderful to teach prosperity, as long as it is understood that the Church is not an elite organization for spiritual yuppies only, one that excludes other social classes.

If uniqueness is to be appreciated racially and socially, it is certainly to be appreciated sexually. Male and female are one in Christ. Yet they are unique, and that uniqueness is not to be tampered with. Let the male be masculine and the female be feminine! It is a sin for a man to misrepresent himself by conducting himself as a woman. I am not merely speaking of homosexuality. I am also talking about men who are feminine in their mannerisms. Many of these men may not be homosexual in their behavior, but the Bible says that they must be healed of feminine mannerisms. It is equally sad to see a masculine woman. Nevertheless, God wants them healed, not hated!

> *Know ye not that the unrighteous shall not inherit the kingdom of God? Be not deceived: neither fornicators, nor idolaters, nor adulterers, nor effeminate, nor abusers of themselves with mankind...*(1 Corinthians 6:9).

I realize that these behavioral disorders are areas that require healing and prayer. My point

is simply that unity does not negate uniqueness. God is saying, "I don't want men to lose
their masculine uniqueness." This is true
racially, socially, and sexually. God can appreciate our differences and still create unity. It
is like a conductor who can orchestrate
extremely different instruments into produc-
ing a harmonious, unified sound. Together we
produce a sound of harmony that expresses
the multifaceted character of God.

Having established the uniqueness of unity,
let us now discuss some aspects of the uniqueness of the woman. By nature a woman is a
receiver. She is not physically designed to be a
giver. Her sexual and emotional fulfillment
becomes somewhat dependent on the giving of her
male counterpart (in regard to intimate relationships). There is a certain vulnerability that is a
part of being a receiver. In regard to reproduction
(sexual relationships), the man is the contributing factor, and the woman is the receiver.

What is true of the natural is true of the
spiritual. Men tend to act out of what they per-
ceive to be facts, while women tend to react out
of their emotions. If your actions and moods are
not a reaction to the probing of the Holy Spirit,
then you are reacting to the subtle taunting of
the enemy. He is trying to produce his destructive fruit in your home, heart, and even in your

relationships. Receiver, be careful what you receive! Moods and attitudes that satan would offer, you need to resist. Tell the enemy, "This is not me, and I don't receive it." It is his job to offer it and your job to resist it. If you do your job, all will go well.

> *Men tend to act out what they perceive as facts.*

Submit yourselves, then, to God. Resist the devil, and he will flee from you (James 4:7 NIV).

Don't allow the enemy to plug into you and violate you through his subtle seductions. He is a giver and he is looking for a receiver. You must discern his influence if you are going to rebuke him. Anything that comes, or any mood that is not in agreement with God's Word, is satan trying to plug into the earthly realm through your life. He wants you to believe you cannot change. He loves prisons and chains! Statements like, "This is just the way I am," or "I am in a terrible mood today," come from lips that accept what they ought to reject. Never allow yourself to settle for anything less than the attitude God wants you to have in your heart. Don't let satan have your day, your husband, or your home. Eve could have put the devil out!

Neither give place to the devil (Ephesians 4:27).

It is not enough to reject the enemy's plan. You must nurture the Word of the Lord. You need to draw the promise of God and the vision for the future to your breast. It is a natural law that anything not fed will die. Whatever you have drawn to the breast is what is growing in your life. Breast-feeding holds several advantages for what you feed: (a) It hears your heart beat; (b) It is warmed by your closeness; (c) It draws nourishment from you. Caution: Be sure you are nurturing what you want to grow and starving what you want to die.

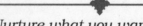

> *Nurture what you want to grow;*
> *starve what you want to die.*

As you read this, you may feel that life is passing you by. You often experience success in one area and gross defeat in others. You need a burning desire for the future, the kind of desire that overcomes past fears and inhibitions. You will remain chained to your past and all the secrets therein, until you decide: Enough is

Infirmed Woman

enough! I am telling you that when your desire for the future peaks, you can break out of prison. I challenge you to sit down and write 30 things you would like to do with your life and scratch them off, one by one, as you accomplish them. There is no way you can plan for the future and dwell in the past at the same time. I feel an earthquake coming into your prison! It is midnight the turning point of days! It is your time for a change. Praise God and escape out of the dungeons of your past.

> *And at midnight Paul and Silas prayed, and sang praises unto God: and the prisoners heard them. And suddenly there was a great earthquake, so that the foundations of the prison were shaken: and immediately all the doors were opened, and every one's bands were loosed* (Acts 16:25-26).

Have you ever noticed how hard it is to communicate with people who will not give you their attention? Pain will not continue to rehearse itself in the life of a preoccupied, distracted person. Distracted people almost seem weird. They do not respond! Every woman has something she wishes she could forget. There is a principle to learn here. Forgetting isn't a memory lapse; it is a memory release! Like carbon dioxide the

149

body can no longer use, exhale it and let it go out of your spirit.

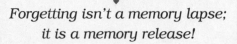

*Forgetting isn't a memory lapse;
it is a memory release!*

Brethren, I count not myself to have apprehended: but this one thing I do, forgetting those things which are behind, and reaching forth unto those things which are before, I press toward the mark for the prize of the high calling of God in Christ Jesus. Let us therefore, as many as be perfect, be thus minded: and if in any thing ye be otherwise minded, God shall reveal even this unto you (Philippians 3:13-15).

Jesus set the infirmed woman free. She was able to stand upright. The crippling condition of her infirmity was removed by the God who cares, sees, and calls the infirmity to the dispensary of healing and deliverance. You can call upon Him even in the middle of the night. Like a 24-hour medical center, you can reach Him at anytime. He is touched by the feeling of your infirmity.

For we have not an high priest which cannot be touched with the feeling of our infirmities; but was in all points tempted like as we are, yet without sin (Hebrews 4:15).

In the name of our High Priest, Jesus Christ, *I curse the infirmity that has bowed the backs of God's women.* I pray that, as we share together out of the Word of God, the Holy Spirit would roll you into the recovery room where you can fully realize that the trauma is over. I am excited to say that God never loosed anybody that He wasn't going to use mightily. May God reveal healing and purpose, as we continue to seek Him.

Thoughts and Reflections

_____
_____
_____
_____
_____
_____
_____
_____
_____
_____
_____
_____
_____
_____
_____
_____
_____
_____
_____
_____
_____

Chapter 1

Can You Stand to be Blessed?
The Transformers

*B*ut as many as received Him, to
them gave He power to become the
sons of God, even to them that believe on
His name (John 1:12).

I pray that we as Christians never lose our
conviction that God does change lives. We must
protect this message. Our God enables us to
make the radical changes necessary for fulfilling our purposes and responsibilities. Like the
caterpillar that eats and sleeps its way into
change, the process occurs gradually, but

nonetheless powerfully. Many people who will rock this world are sleeping in the cocoon of obscurity, waiting for their change to come. The Scriptures declare, "...it is high time to awake out of sleep: for now is our salvation nearer than when we believed" (Rom. 13:11).

A memory of my twin sons playing on the floor when they were children tailors the continuity of this text for me. They were playing with a truck, contributing all the sounds of grinding gears and roaring engines. I didn't pay much attention, as I began unwinding from the day's stresses and challenges. Distractedly, I glanced down at the floor and noticed that the boys were now running an airplane down an imaginary runway. I asked, "What happened to the truck you were playing with?" They explained, "Daddy, this is a transformer!" I then inquired, "What is a transformer?" Their answer brought me into the Presence of the Lord. They said, "It can be transformed from what it was before into whatever we want it to be!"

Suddenly I realized that God had made the first transformer! He created man from dust. He created him in such a way that, if need be, He could pull a woman out of him without ever having to reach back into the dust. Out of one creative act God transformed the man into a marriage. Then He transformed the marriage into a family, the family into a society, etc. God never had to reach into the ground again because the power to transform was intrinsically placed into man. All types of potential were locked into our spirits before birth. For the Christian, transformation at its optimum is the outworking of the internal. God placed certain things in us that must come out. We house the prophetic power of God. Every word of our personal prophetic destiny is inside us. He has ordained us to be!

> *Every word of our personal prophetic destiny is inside us.*

Before I formed thee in the belly I knew thee; and before thou camest forth out of the womb I sanctified thee, and I ordained thee a prophet unto the nations (Jeremiah 1:5).

Only when we are weary from trying to unlock our own resources do we come to the Lord, receive Him, and allow Him to release in us the power to become whatever we need to be. Actually, isn't that what we want to know—our purpose? Then we can use the power to become who we really are. Life has chiseled many of us into mere fragments of who we were meant to be. To all who receive Him, Christ gives them the power to slip out of who they were forced to become, so that they can transform into the individuals they each were created to be.

Salvation, as it relates to destiny, is the God-given power to become what God has eternally decreed you were before. "Before what?" you ask; before the foundation of the world. What Christians so often refer to as "grace" truly is God's divine enablement to accomplish predestined purpose. When the Lord says to Paul, "My grace is sufficient for thee..." (2 Cor. 12:9), He is simply stating that His power is not intimidated by circumstances. You are empowered by God to reach and accomplish goals that transcend human limitations! It is important that each and every vessel God uses realize that they were able to accomplish what others could not only because God gave them the grace to do so. Problems are not really problems to a person who has the grace to serve in a particular area.

How many times have people walked up to me and said, "I don't see how you can stand this or that." If God has given us the grace to operate in a certain situation, those things do not affect us as they would someone else who does not have the grace to function in that area. Therefore, it is important that we not imitate other people. Assuming that we may be equally talented, we still may not be equally graced. Remember, God always empowers whomever He employs. Ultimately, we must realize that the excellency of our gifts are of God and not of us. He doesn't need nearly as much of our contributions as we think He does. So it is God who works out the internal destinies of men. He gives us the power to become who we are eternally and internally.

> *Wherefore, My beloved, as ye have always obeyed, not as in My presence only, but now much more in My absence, work out your own salvation with fear and trembling. For it is God which worketh in you both to will and to do of His good pleasure* (Philippians 2:12-13).

Today, in the Body of Christ a great deal of emphasis is placed on the process of mentoring. The concept of mentoring is both scriptural and effective; however, as we often do, many of us have gone to extremes. Instead of teaching young men to pursue God, the ultimate Rabbi, they are running amuck looking for a man to pour into them. All men are not mentored as

Joshua was—under the firm hand of a strong leader. Some, like Moses, are prepared by the workings of the manifold wisdom of God. This latter group receives mentoring through the carefully orchestrated circumstances that God ordains to accomplish an end result. Regardless of which describes your ascent to greatness, it is still God who "worketh in you both to will and to do..." (Phil. 2:13). When you understand this, you appreciate the men or the methods God used, but ultimately praise the God, whose masterful ability to conduct, has crescendoed in the finished product of a man or woman of God.

> *And the Lord said unto Moses, Gather unto Me seventy men of the elders of Israel, whom thou knowest to be the elders of the people, and officers over them; and bring them unto the tabernacle of the congregation, that they may stand there with thee* (Numbers 11:16).

In keeping with this mentoring concept, let's consider Moses' instructions when asked to consecrate elders in Israel. I found it interesting that God told Moses to gather unto Him men whom he knew were elders. God says, "I want you to separate men to be elders who are elders." You can only ordain a man to be what he already is. The insight we need to succeed is the discernment of who is among us. Woe unto the man who is placed into what he is not. Moses was to bring these men into a full circle. In other words, they were to be led into what they already were. Perhaps this will further clarify my point: When the prodigal son was in the "hog pen," it was said, "And when he came to himself..." (Luke 15:17). We are fulfilled only when we are led into being who we were predestined to be. Real success is *coming to ourselves.*

The thing that gives individuals the power to arise above their circumstances is coming to themselves. You feel fulfilled, when you achieve a sense of belonging through your job, family, or ministry. Have you ever met anyone who left you with a feeling of familiarity—almost as if you had known the person? A sense of bonding comes out of similarities. Likewise, there are certain jobs or ministries that feel comfortable, even if they are tasks you have never done before. If you are discerning, you can feel a sense of belonging in certain situations. However, weary are the legs of a traveler who cannot find his way home. Spiritual wanderings plague the lives of many people who wrestle with discontentment. May God grant you success in finding your way to a sense of wholeness and completion.

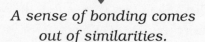

A sense of bonding comes out of similarities.

Change is a gift from God. It is given to the person who finds himself too far removed from what he feels destiny has ordained for him. There is nothing wrong with being wrong, but there is something wrong with not making the necessary adjustments to get things right! Even within the Christian community, some do not believe in God's ability to change the human heart. This unbelief in God's ability to change causes people to judge others on the basis of their past. Dead issues are periodically revived in the mouths of gossips. Still, the Lord progressively regenerates the minds of His children. Don't assume that real change occurs without struggle and prayer. However, change can be achieved.

God exalted Him to His own right hand as Prince and Savior that He might give repentance and forgiveness of sins to Israel (Acts 5:31 NIV).

The Bible calls change *repentance*. Repentance is God's gift to a struggling heart who wants to find himself. The Lord wants to bring you to a place of safety and shelter. Without the Holy Spirit's help you can search and search and still not find repentance. The Lord will show the place of repentance only to those who hunger and thirst after righteousness. One moment with the Spirit of God can lead you into a place of renewal that, on your own, you would not find or enjoy. I believe it was this kind of grace that made John Newton record, "It was grace that taught my heart to fear and grace my fears relieved. How precious did that grace appear the hour I first believed" (*Amazing Grace*, early American melody). When God gives you the grace to make changes that you know you couldn't do with your own strength, it becomes precious to you.

> *For ye know how that afterward, when he would have inherited the blessing, he was rejected: for he found no place of repentance, though he sought it carefully with tears* (Hebrews 12:17).

Brother Esau sought for the place of repentance and could not secure it. To be transformed is to be changed. If you are not moving into your divine purpose, you desperately need to repent. "Repent" has a strong negative connotation for the person indoctrinated to believe that repentance is a fearful and dangerous action. It is not dangerous. Repentance is the prerequisite of revival. There cannot be revival without prayerful repentance. John the Baptist taught Israel, "Repent ye: for the kingdom of heaven is at hand" (Matt. 3:2). If God wants you to change, it is because He wants you to be prepared for what He desires to do next in your life. Get ready; the best is yet to come.

> *Repentance is the*
> *prerequisite of revival.*

For whom He did foreknow, He also did predestinate to be conformed to the image of His Son, that He might be the firstborn among many brethren (Romans 8:29).

And be not conformed to this world: but be ye transformed by the renewing of your mind, that ye may prove what is that good, and acceptable, and perfect, will of God (Romans 12:2).

Now let's deal with some real issues! The word "conformed" in Romans 8:29 is *summorphoo* (Strong's #4832), which means "to be fashioned like or shaped into the image or the picture" of—in this case—Christ. God has predestined you to shape up into a picture of Christ in the earth. Christ is the firstborn of a huge family of siblings who all bear a striking resemblance to their Father. The shaping of a will, however, requires a visit to the garden of Gethsemane. *Gethsemane* literally means "oil press" (Strong's #1068). God presses the oil of His anointing out of your life through adversity. When you forsake your will in order to be shaped into a clearer picture of Christ, you will see little drops of oil coming out in your walk and work for God. In short, He predestined the pressing in your life that produces the oil. As you are pressed, you gradually conform to the image of your predestined purpose.

As you are pressed, you gradually conform to your purpose.

In Romans 12:2 we are instructed not to be conformed to this world. Literally, it says we are not to be conformed to the same pattern of this world. The text warns us against submitting to the dictates of the world. We are to avoid using those standards as a pattern for our progress. On a deeper level God is saying, "Do not use the same pattern of the world to measure success or to establish character and values." The term "world" in Greek is *aion* (Strong's #165), which refers to ages. Together, these words tell us, "Do not allow the pattern of the times you are in to become the pattern that shapes your inward person."

At this point I can almost hear someone saying, "How do you respond to the preexisting circumstances and conditions that have greatly affected you?" Or, "I am already shaped into something less than what God would want me to be because of the times in which I live, or the circumstances in which I grew up." I am glad you asked these things. You see, every aspect of your being that has already been conformed to this age must be transformed! The prefix *trans* implies movement, as in the words *transport, translate, transact, transition,* and so forth. In this light, *transform* would imply moving the form. On a deeper level, it means "moving from one form into another," as in the tadpole that is transformed into the frog and the

caterpillar into the butterfly. No matter what
has disfigured you, in God is the power to be
transformed.

Many individuals in the Body of Christ are
persevering without progressing. They wrestle
with areas that have been conformed to the
world instead of transformed. This is particularly true of us Pentecostals who often
emphasize the gifts of the Spirit and exciting
services. It is imperative that, while we keep
our mode of expression, we understand that
transformation doesn't come from inspiration!
Many times preachers sit down after ministering a very inspiring sermon feeling that they
accomplished more than they actually did.
Transformation takes place in the mind.

The Bible teaches that we are to be
renewed by the transforming of our minds (see
Rom. 12:2; Eph. 4:23). Only the Holy Spirit
knows how to renew the mind. The struggle we
have inside us is with our self-perception.
Generally, our perception of ourselves is
affected by those around us. Our early opin-
ion of ourselves is deeply affected by the
opinions of the authoritative figures in our
formative years. If our parents tend to neglect
or ignore us, it tears at our self-worth. Eventually, though, we mature to the degree where we
can walk in the light of our own self-image,

without it being diluted by the contributions of others.

> *Our perception of ourselves is affected by those around us.*

When we experience the new birth, we again go back to the formative years of being deeply impressionable. It's important to be discerning in who we allow to influence us in the early years. Whenever we become intimate with someone, the first thing we should want to know is, "Who do you say that I am?" Our basic need is to be understood by the inner circle of people with whom we walk. However, we must be ready to abort negative, destructive information that doesn't bring us into an accelerated awareness of inner realities and strengths. Jesus was able to ask Peter, "Who do you say that I am?" because He already knew the answer! (See Matthew 16:15.) To ask someone to define you, without first knowing the answer within yourself, is dangerous. When we ask that kind of question, without an inner awareness, we open the door for manipulation. In short, Jesus knew who He was.

The Lord wants to help you realize who you are and what you are graced to do. When you understand that He is the only One who really knows you, then you pursue Him with fierceness and determination. Pursue Him! Listen to what Paul shares at the meeting on Mars' Hill.

> *And hath made of one blood all nations of men for to dwell on all the face of the earth, and hath determined the times before appointed, and the bounds of their habitation; that they should seek the Lord, if haply they might feel after Him, and find Him, though He be not far from every one of us: for in Him we live, and move, and have our being; as certain also of your own poets have said, For we are also His offspring* (Acts 17:26-28).

The basic message of this passage is that God has set the bounds on our habitations. He knows who we are and how we are to attain. This knowledge, locked up in the counsel of God's omniscience, is the basis of our pursuit, and it is the release of that knowledge that brings immediate transformation. He knows the hope or the goal of our calling. He is not far removed from us; He reveals Himself to people who seek Him. The finders are the seekers. The door is opened only to the knockers and the gifts are given to the askers! (See Luke 11:9.) Initiation is our responsibility. Whosoever hungers and thirsts shall be filled. Remember, in every crisis He is never far from the seeker!

Transforming truths are brought forth through the birth canal of our diligence in seeking His face. It is while you are in His presence that He utters omniscient insights into your individual purpose and course. Jesus told a woman who had been wrestling with a crippling condition for 18 years that she was not really bound—that in fact she was loosed! Immediately she was transformed by the renewing of her mind. (See Luke 13:11-13.) It is no wonder David said, "In Thy presence is fulness of joy" (Ps. 16:11b). The answer is in the Presence—the Presence of God, not man! There is a renewing word that will change your mind about your circumstances. Just when the enemy thinks he has you, transform before his very eyes!

No matter who left his impression upon you, God's Word prevails! The obstacles of past scars can be overcome by present truths. Your deliverance will not start in your circumstances; it will always evolve out of your mentality. As the Word of God waxes greater, the will of men becomes weaker. Paul said in Ephesians 5:26 that Jesus cleanses by the "washing of water by the Word...." So turn the faucet on high and ease your mind down into the sudsy warm water of profound truth. Gently wash away every limitation and residue of past obstacles, and gradually, luxuriously, transform into the refreshed, renewed person you were created to become. Whenever someone tells you what you can't do or be, or what you can't get or attain, then tell them, "I can do all things through Christ who strengthens me! I am a transformer!" (See Philippians 4:13 and Romans 12:2.)

The obstacles of past scars can be overcome by present truths.

Thoughts and Reflections

_____

_____

_____

_____

_____

_____

_____

_____

_____

_____

_____

_____

_____

_____

_____

_____

_____

_____

_____

_____

Other Books
by T.D. Jakes

Woman, Thou Art Loosed!

Naked and Not Ashamed

Hope for Every Moment

Can You Stand to be Blessed?

Why? Because You Are Anointed

Why? Because You Are Anointed Workbook

Help Me, I've Fallen and I Can't Get Up!

When Shepherds Bleed

Water in the Wilderness

The Harvest Workbook

The Great Investment

Maximize the Moment